CAMPAIGN • 214

# THE CORAL SEA 1942

## The first carrier battle

**MARK STILLE**

ILLUSTRATED BY JOHN WHITE

*Series editors Marcus Cowper and Nikolai Bogdanovic*

First published in Great Britain in 2009 by Osprey Publishing,
Midland House, West Way, Botley, Oxford OX2 0PH, UK
443 Park Avenue South, New York, NY 10016, USA
E-mail: info@ospreypublishing.com

A CIP catalog record for this book is available from the British Library.

ISBN: 978 1 84603 440 4
E book ISBN: 978 1 84908 106 1

Editorial by Ilios Publishing Ltd, Oxford, UK (www.iliospublishing.com)

Page layout by: Ken Vail Graphic Design
Index by Michael Forder
Typeset in Myriad Pro and Sabon
Maps by Bounford.com
3D bird's-eye views by Ian Palmer
Battlescene illustrations by John White
Originated by PPS Grasmere Ltd
Printed in China through Worldprint

09   10   11   12   13   10 9 8 7 6 5 4 3 2 1

## THE WOODLAND TRUST

Osprey Publishing are supporting the Woodland Trust, the UK's leading
woodland conservation charity, by funding the dedication of trees.

FOR A CATALOG OF ALL BOOKS PUBLISHED BY OSPREY MILITARY
AND AVIATION PLEASE CONTACT:

Osprey Direct, c/o Random House Distribution Center,
400 Hahn Road, Westminster, MD 21157
Email: uscustomerservice@ospreypublishing.com

Osprey Direct, The Book Service Ltd, Distribution Centre,
Colchester Road, Frating Green, Colchester, Essex, CO7 7DW
E-mail: customerservice@ospreypublishing.com

**www.ospreypublishing.com**

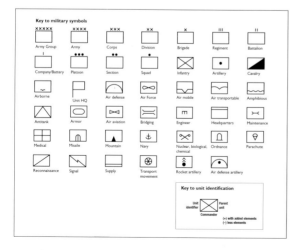

## AUTHOR'S DEDICATION

This book is dedicated to Louise who aided and abetted my passion
for writing.

## AUTHOR'S ACKNOWLEDGMENTS

The author is indebted to the staffs of the US Naval Historical Center
Photographic Section and the Yamato Museum (formerly the Kure Maritime
Museum) and to Tohru Kizu, editor of *Ships of the World Magazine*, for their
assistance in procuring the photographs used in this title.

# CONTENTS

# Strategic situation, May 1942

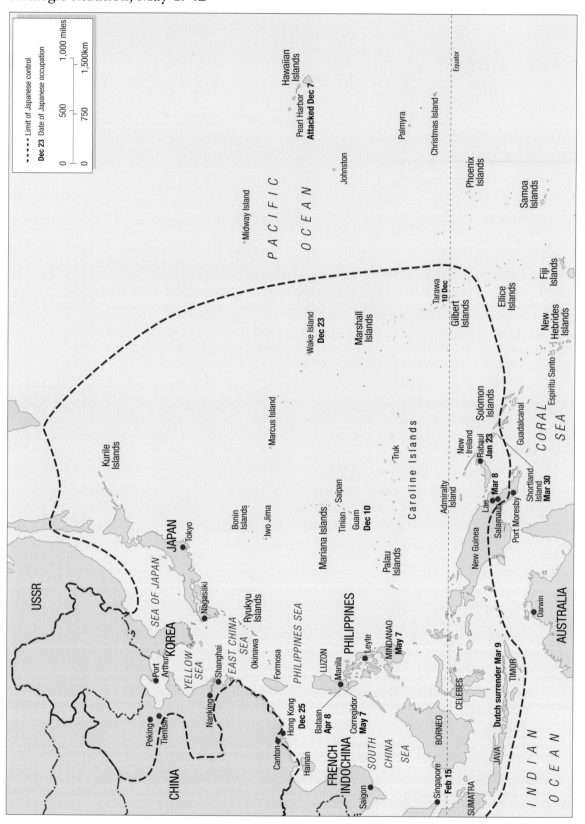

**Legend:**
- ▪▪▪▪▪ Limit of Japanese control
- **Dec 23** Date of Japanese occupation

Scale:
0 — 500 — 1,000 miles
0 — 750 — 1,500km

USSR

CHINA

Peking
Tientsin

Port Arthur

Nanking

Shanghai

KOREA

JAPAN
Tokyo

Nagasaki

SEA OF JAPAN

YELLOW SEA

EAST CHINA SEA

Okinawa
Ryukyu Islands

Formosa

Canton

Hong Kong
**Dec 25**

Hainan

FRENCH INDOCHINA

Saigon

Singapore
**Feb 15**

SOUTH CHINA SEA

SUMATRA

BORNEO

JAVA
**Dutch surrender Mar 9**

CELEBES

TIMOR

Darwin

AUSTRALIA

INDIAN OCEAN

PHILIPPINES SEA

LUZON

Manila

Corregidor
**May 7**

Bataan
**Apr 8**

MINDANAO
**May 7**

Leyte

PHILIPPINES

Palau Islands

Mariana Islands

Tinian · Saipan
Guam
**Dec 10**

Bonin Islands

Iwo Jima

Kurile Islands

Caroline Islands

Truk

Marcus Island

Wake Island
**Dec 23**

Midway Island

PACIFIC OCEAN

Marshall Islands

Johnston

Hawaiian Islands

Pearl Harbor
**Attacked Dec 7**

Palmyra

Christmas Island

Equator

Phoenix Islands

Samoa Islands

Fiji Islands

Ellice Islands

Gilbert Islands

Tarawa
**10 Dec**

New Hebrides Islands

Espiritu Santo

CORAL SEA

Guadalcanal

Solomon Islands

Shortland Island
**Mar 30**

Rabaul
**Jan 23**

New Ireland

New Britain

Admiralty Island

New Guinea

Lae

Salamaua
**Mar 8**

Port Moresby

# ORIGINS OF THE CAMPAIGN

The great Pacific War between The United States and Japan opened in a totally unexpected fashion. For the US Navy, the attack on Pearl Harbor on December 7, 1941, resulted in the destruction of its Pacific Fleet. Of the eight battleships present, five ended the day either blown apart or resting on the mud of Pearl Harbor. Instead of a great naval clash somewhere in the Western Pacific during the course of the American drive toward Japan, the US Navy was not in a position to contest Japanese expansion throughout the Pacific. Fortunately for the Americans, none of the Pacific Fleet's aircraft carriers were present at Pearl Harbor. With these ships, and an entirely new doctrine, the US Navy pondered how to reverse the tide of Japanese expansion.

Even the Imperial Japanese Navy (IJN) was caught unaware by its success at Pearl Harbor. The concept of massing all of the fleet's large carriers into a single cohesive unit, combined with the excellent aircraft and superb aircrews of the carriers themselves, had created a revolution in naval warfare. The destruction of the American battlefleet had clearly demonstrated that air power was now the dominant factor in naval warfare. As with the Americans,

*Shokaku* in August 1941 just after completion. She was the lead ship in the most successful Japanese carrier design of the war. After being damaged at the Coral Sea, she went on to see action in the carrier battles at Eastern Solomons and Santa Cruz until finally being sunk by submarine attack in the climactic carrier battle at the Philippine Sea. (US Naval Historical Center)

After Pearl Harbor and up until the battle of the Coral Sea, the Pacific Fleet's carriers engaged in a number of raids on Japanese-held islands. The offensive strategy was the brainchild of Admiral King, but did little damage to the Japanese. *Yorktown* is shown here on February 6, 1942, returning to Pearl Harbor after the Marshalls–Gilberts raid. This view is taken from *Enterprise* and show's *Yorktown's* crew at quarters in dress whites as the ship enters port. (US Naval Historical Center)

this development rendered the IJN's pre-war calculations irrelevant. The IJN was also built for a decisive clash of dreadnoughts for mastery of the Pacific, but this clash would never occur. However, with its decided edge in aircraft carriers, the IJN could now conduct a war of expansion with the hopes that it could construct an unassailable position in the Pacific.

Japanese expansion in the Pacific was conducted under a plan agreed to by the IJN and Army. This called for a series of sequenced operations designed to bring key areas under Japanese control in order to construct the "Greater East Asian Co-Prosperity Sphere." Once these areas were consolidated and defended, Japan would be in a good position, according to the plan, to negotiate a peace with the United States which would be unprepared and unwilling to pay the price required to remove Japan from her new conquests. As laid out by Imperial Headquarters, the initial part of the war was divided into two "operational stages." The first operational stage called for the occupation of the Philippines, Malaya, the Dutch East Indies, Burma and Rabaul. One of the hallmarks of the early campaigns was the virtually uncontested success of the IJN's carrier force or Kido Butai. Following the Pearl Harbor operation, the Kido Butai was used to cover the capture of Rabaul in January 1942 and the Dutch East Indies in February. In April, Japanese carriers moved into the Indian Ocean to conduct a rampage against British naval forces and shipping.

As the Japanese sought to achieve their first operational stage objectives, Allied naval forces were unable to stop the Japanese advance. In the first large surface ship action of the war at the battle of the Java Sea, an Allied naval force was shattered by a Japanese force of similar size demonstrating the superiority of the IJN's destroyer and cruiser forces. Not wanting to be totally defensive, but unable to oppose the massed Japanese carriers, the US Navy began a series of carrier strikes in the Central Pacific. The first action was conducted by the carriers *Enterprise* and *Yorktown* against the Marshall and Gilbert islands on February 1, 1942. The *Enterprise* hit targets in the northern Marshalls while the *Yorktown* hit targets in the Marshalls and in the northern Gilberts. Damage to the Japanese was light, despite the claims of US aviators. The *Enterprise* followed with strikes on Wake Island on February 24 and Marcus Island on March 4, 1942. The first US carrier action with strategic results was the Lae–Salamaua raid on March 10, 1942, by the carriers *Yorktown* and *Lexington*. Following Japanese landings at these points on the island of New Guinea, aircraft from the two carriers hit Japanese shipping remaining in the area. Again, the Americans made claims of inflicting great damage, and this time there was some substance to the claims. The damage inflicted by the two carriers was sufficient to make the Japanese pause until they could muster a carrier escort for their next move. Thus, the proposed operation against the strategic airfield at Port Moresby on New Guinea was postponed until the Japanese could provide their own carriers to support the operation.

Meanwhile, the carriers *Enterprise* and *Hornet* were committed to the raid on Tokyo, which was conducted on April 16. Whatever the psychological results were for American morale or for Japanese fears of further raids on their homeland, the commitment of half of the Pacific Fleet's carriers to this

Among the Japanese ships suffering damage during the Lae–Salamaua raid was the seaplane tender *Kiyokawa Maru*, shown here. The arrow just visible points to bomb damage on the ship. Several floatplanes are also visible. *Kiyokawa Maru*'s damage prevented her from taking part in the MO Operation, but her aircraft embarked on seaplane tender *Kamikawa Maru*. (US Naval Historical Center)

8YK, 3-10-42 FL: 6 3/8" ALT: TAKEN DURING ACTION

The March 10 raid by carriers *Lexington* and *Yorktown* on Japanese shipping off Lae–Salamaua was the heaviest damage yet inflicted on the IJN in a single day in the war. Despite extravagant claims by American aviators, actual Japanese losses were heavy enough with an auxiliary cruiser, one transport and a converted minesweeper sunk. The 8,624-ton auxiliary cruiser *Kongo Maru* is shown sinking in this shot taken by a VS-5 Dauntless from *Yorktown*. The American raid set in motion a chain of events leading to the carrier battle of the Coral Sea. (US Naval Historical Center)

operation meant that they could not respond to the next Japanese offensive move in the South Pacific in early May. During the second operational stage, the Japanese envisioned further expansion into eastern New Guinea, New Britain, the Fijis and Samoa in the South Pacific. With the Japanese now ready to execute these plans, the unavailability of the *Enterprise* and *Hornet* meant that the commander of the Pacific Fleet could deploy only two carriers to the South Pacific by the time the Japanese offensive was predicted to begin in early May. With part of the Kido Butai committed to support the South Pacific operation, the scene was set for history's first carrier battle.

# CHRONOLOGY

**1941**

**December 7**    Japanese carrier force (Kido Butai) attacks Pearl Harbor, Hawaii, and cripples the Pacific Fleet's battle line. No American carriers are in port.

**1942**

**January 23**    Kido Butai supports Japanese seizure of Rabaul on island of New Britain.

**February 1**    US carriers conduct Marshalls–Gilberts raid.

**February 19**    Kido Butai raids Darwin in northern Australia.

**February 24**    The US carrier *Enterprise* conducts raid on Wake Island.

**February 25 to March 10**    Kido Butai supports invasion of Java in Dutch East Indies.

**February 27**    Battle of Java Sea; Allied surface forces unable to prevent invasion of Java.

**March 4**    The *Enterprise* raids Marcus Island.

**March 10**    American carrier aircraft strike Japanese naval forces at Lae and Salamaua on New Guinea. Further Japanese expansion into South Pacific halted until IJN can provide carrier cover.

**March 26 to April 18**    Kido Butai conducts Indian Ocean Raid.

**April 16**    The carriers *Enterprise* and *Hornet* conduct Tokyo raid. This means they will be unavailable for operations in the Coral Sea when Japanese launch next offensive in South Pacific.

**April 29**    Tulagi Invasion Force departs Rabaul.

**April 29**    MO Main Body departs Truk.

**May 1**    MO Carrier Striking Force departs Truk.

**May 2**    MO Carrier Striking Force unable to deliver fighter aircraft to Rabaul.

**May 3**    Tulagi occupied by Japanese.

| | | |
|---|---|---|
| **May 3** | | MO Carrier Striking Force fails in its second attempt to deliver fighter aircraft to Rabaul; falls two days behind schedule. |
| **May 4** | | The carrier *Yorktown* raids Japanese invasion shipping off Tulagi. |
| **May 4** | | MO Invasion Force departs Rabaul. |
| **May 5** | | MO Carrier Striking Force enters the Coral Sea; US carriers located south of Guadalcanal. |
| **May 6** | 1030hrs | Japanese flying boat spots US carriers; MO Carrier Striking Force unable to react. |
| **May 7** | 0722hrs | *Shokaku* search aircraft reports US carriers south of MO Carrier Striking Force. |
| | 0815hrs | US carrier aircraft report two Japanese carriers north of Misima Island. |
| | 0900hrs | Japanese strike reaches area of reported carrier contact and finds only an oiler and a destroyer. |
| | 1000hrs | Japanese carrier dive-bombers sink a destroyer; oiler damaged and sinks days later. |
| | 1110hrs | American carrier aircraft locate and attack the Japanese light carrier *Shoho*. |
| | 1135hrs | The *Shoho* sinks after massive bomb and torpedo damage with heavy loss of life. |
| **May 8** | 0820hrs | MO Carrier Striking Force spotted by American carrier aircraft. |
| | 0822hrs | American carriers sighted by Japanese carrier aircraft. |
| | 0925hrs | US carrier air strikes depart. |
| | 0930hrs | Japanese carrier air strike departs. |
| | 1100hrs | *Yorktown* aircraft begin dive-bombing attack on the Japanese carrier *Shokaku*. |
| | 1105hrs | First of two bomb hits on the *Shokaku*; Japanese carrier is not sunk but is forced to leave battle. |
| | 1118hrs | Japanese carrier torpedo planes attack the *Yorktown* with no success. |
| | 1118hrs | Japanese carrier torpedo planes attack the *Lexington*. |
| | 1120hrs | First of two torpedoes hits the *Lexington*. |
| | 1121hrs | Japanese carrier dive-bombers attack the *Lexington* and score two hits. Damage is light. |
| | 1124hrs | Japanese carrier dive-bombers attack the *Yorktown* scoring a single hit. Damage is moderate, but the *Yorktown* can continue to operate aircraft. |
| | 1142hrs | *Lexington* aircraft attack the *Shokaku*. One additional bomb hit is scored. |
| | 1315hrs | Fletcher decides to retire; TF-17 moves south. |
| | 1620hrs | Inoue postpones MO Operation. |
| | 1952hrs | The *Lexington* sinks as a result of gasoline vapor explosions caused by torpedo damage. |

# OPPOSING COMMANDERS

## THE IJN

The most important figure in determining Japanese naval strategy was **Admiral Yamamoto Isoroku**. Yamamoto was a complex individual known for his aggressive nature and gambler's instincts. He had been an early convert to the rising importance of naval air power and had commanded the carrier *Akagi* and then a carrier division. Unusual for an IJN officer, he had spent significant time in the US between the wars and had first-hand opportunity to observe and respect America's tremendous industrial potential. Yamamoto was appointed commander-in-chief of the Combined Fleet in September 1939. Although he was not in favor of going to war with the US, his strategic concepts helped shape the early course of the conflict. Despite intense opposition, he was the driving force behind the Pearl Harbor operation. By early 1942, Yamamoto's primacy in shaping Japanese naval strategy was assured. Admiral Nagano Osami, Chief of the Naval General Staff, was the nominal head of the IJN and should have been its primary figure for shaping strategy, but the undisputed success of Yamamoto's Pearl Harbor gamble and his readiness to threaten to resign in order to get his way made him the real arbiter of Japanese naval strategy. Despite his opposition to further operations in the South Pacific, which he viewed as contrary to his preferred Central Pacific drive in order to bring the US Pacific Fleet to a decisive battle, Yamamoto grudgingly gave his approval to the attack on Port Moresby and even contributed a significant proportion of the Kido Butai. This act was to have massive consequences for not only the Coral Sea battle, but also for the subsequent battle of Midway.

**Vice Admiral Inoue Shigeyoshi** was commander of the 4th Fleet, also know as the South Sea Force. He was the former chief of the Aeronautical Department and was therefore fully aware of the role aircraft now played in naval warfare. He aggressively pushed to expand Japan's operations in the South Pacific and as such, he was the designer of the Japanese operations into the Coral Sea.

**Rear Admiral Takagi Takeo** was commander of the MO Carrier Striking Force. He was promoted to vice admiral during the battle with an effective date of May 1. Early in his career he was a submarine specialist, but in 1937 transitioned to the surface navy. He gained flag rank in November 1938 and was appointed commander of the 5th Cruiser Division (which consisted of the IJN's four powerful *Myoko*-class units) in September 1941. In this capacity, he was the commander of the Japanese covering force that engaged and defeated

Vice Admiral Takagi Takeo was charged with the most important role in the MO Operation as commander of the MO Carrier Striking Force. He squandered several chances to deal a devastating blow to the American carriers and ultimately failed either to protect the Invasion Force or destroy the American carriers. After the Coral Sea, he was assigned secondary commands until June 1943 when he was given command of the 6th Fleet (submarines). He was killed on Saipan in July 1944. (US Naval Institute)

Allied forces in the battle of the Java Sea on February 27. By the time of the Coral Sea operation, he remained as commander of the 5th Cruiser Division and, when this force was assigned to the MO Operation, he also became commander of the Carrier Striking Force by virtue of the fact that he was senior to the commander of the 5th Carrier Division. Because Takagi's cruisers were never assigned to work with the IJN's carrier force during the early part of the war, Takagi had no experience with carriers. The unfamiliarity of Takagi and his staff with carrier operations led him to delegate full authority for carrier operations to Hara, the commander of the 5th Carrier Division.

When it came to the carrier battle phase of the Coral Sea battle, **Rear Admiral Hara Chuichi**, commander of the 5th Carrier Division, was the most important Japanese command figure. His fiery nature gave him the nickname "King Kong." He was a surface warfare officer who had gained flag rank in November 1939. However, in September 1941, he was given command of the 5th Carrier Division consisting of the IJN's two newest and most modern carriers. The 5th Carrier Division was assigned to the Kido Butai and took part in the Pearl Harbor attack and the Indian Ocean raid. Thus by May 1942, Hara had accumulated a wealth of carrier experience in a short time.

Commander of the MO Main Body was **Rear Admiral Goto Aritomo**. He had begun the war as commander of Cruiser Squadron 6 (consisting of the IJN's four oldest heavy cruisers of the *Furutaka* and *Aoba* classes) and had conducted operations against Guam, Wake and Rabaul.

The captains of the two primary Japanese carriers present at Coral Sea were not aviators as was customary in the IJN. Yokogawa Ichihei commanded the carrier *Zuikaku* and Jojima Takaji commanded *Shokaku*.

## THE US NAVY

The paramount figure behind all US naval strategy during World War II was **Ernest J. King**. He began his naval career in 1901 upon graduation from the US Naval Academy. His early duties featured both surface ship and submarine billets until he transferred to naval aviation in 1926. He earned his wings in 1927, and assumed command of the carrier *Lexington* in 1930. In 1933, he was promoted to flag rank and was assigned to the Bureau of Aeronautics as its chief. By 1938, he had assumed the rank of vice admiral and was appointed Commander, Aircraft, Battle Force. Much to his disgust, his career looked to be essentially over when he was posted to the General Board (an advisory position seen as a dead end) instead of being selected as Chief of Naval Operations in June 1939.

After a brief period of exile, in January 1941, King's undisputed toughness and leadership skills were recognized and he was appointed as the commander of the Atlantic Fleet. In the command shake-up after Pearl Harbor, King gained more authority as the Commander-in-Chief US Fleet (COMINCH). In March, he was also appointed as Chief of Naval Operations, giving him ultimate authority over all US naval strategy and operations. With this sweeping authority, he quickly sought to expand the Navy's freedom of action in the Pacific, which under the "Germany First" strategy was clearly defined as a secondary theater. It was Ernest King in his position as COMINCH that drove South Pacific strategy in 1941 and into 1942, not the commander of the Pacific Fleet. He was determined to fight for the South Pacific and to begin offensive operations as soon as possible. He did not think that holding key areas in the South Pacific dictated that he conduct a passive defense.

The commander of the US Pacific Fleet, effective December 31, 1941, was **Chester Nimitz**. He graduated from the Naval Academy in 1905 and spent the bulk of his early career associated with submarines. His calm, determined demeanor saw him selected over many more senior admirals to assume the role of Pacific Fleet commander in the aftermath of the Pearl Harbor disaster.

Admiral Chester Nimitz (left) receiving the Distinguished Service Medal from Admiral King aboard the battleship USS *Pennsylvania* on June 30, 1942. The award was given for his leadership of the Pacific Fleet during the battles of the Coral Sea and Midway. (US Naval Historical Center)

Frank Jack Fletcher in the uniform of a vice admiral in September 1942. Despite criticism from many quarters, he was the victor at the battle of the Coral Sea and the first Allied naval commander to inflict a strategic defeat on the Japanese Navy during the Pacific War. (US Naval Historical Center)

On April 3, Nimitz was appointed as commander-in-chief of the Pacific Ocean Areas (including the North Pacific, Central and South Pacific Areas) in addition to his duties as commander of the Pacific Fleet. This meant that Nimitz was responsible for the execution of King's plans to launch offensive operations as soon as possible in the South Pacific region. However, the new command arrangement was not as clean as it appeared. King had set it up so that Nimitz exercised direct control of the Central and North Pacific, but for the South Pacific he had to share command with a Commander, South Pacific Area and Force (Vice Admiral Robert Ghormley). However, by the time of the Coral Sea battle, Ghormley had not arrived so Nimitz exercised authority in the South Pacific.

The role Nimitz played in the lead-up to Coral Sea has been overlooked. After a slow start as commander of the Pacific Fleet, and subjected to constant meddling from King, he seemed unable to assert control of events. By April, things changed. Now his natural aggressiveness began to assert itself and he showed no reluctance to take risks. In response to continued Japanese interest in further expansion in the South Pacific, he pressed King to deploy a second carrier to the region. In an April 25–27 meeting with King, he proposed the bold step of deploying all of the Pacific Fleet's carriers to the South Pacific to set up a major carrier battle. In the end, this bold course of action was approved, but the second pair of carriers could not reach the scene until mid-May.

The most important American naval command personality in the battle was **Rear Admiral Frank Jack Fletcher**. He was a graduate of the US Naval Academy class of 1906 and his initial experience was in destroyers. In 1915, during the US occupation of Vera Cruz, Mexico, he was awarded the Medal of Honor. By the onset of war, he commanded Cruiser Division Six, one of the Scouting Force's three divisions of heavy cruisers. His orders to assume command of the 12 heavy cruisers of the Scouting Force were interrupted by the start of the war. Prior to the war, Fletcher had no experience with aviation. His attempts to transfer to naval aviation were rejected because of bad eyesight. Despite his lack of aviation experience, by the time of Coral Sea, he was one of the US Navy's most seasoned carrier commanders by virtue of several months' experience. In this early point of the war, it was not unusual for non-aviators to command carrier task forces; in fact, this remained commonplace up through November 1942. Fletcher was and remains somewhat of a controversial figure. Both during and after the war, he was criticized for lack of aggressiveness, most notably during the aborted relief operation to Wake Island in December 1941 and in the immediate aftermath of the Guadalcanal landing in August 1942. On balance, it is clear that Fletcher was not afraid of taking risks, but only those he judged could exact a greater price from the enemy. It is interesting to note that the only carrier battle in 1942 that resulted in an American defeat was the only battle fought under a commander other than Fletcher.

Rear Admiral Aubrey Fitch (right) with Rear Admiral John S. McCain in September 1942. Following the Coral Sea, Fitch was assigned as Commander, Aircraft, South Pacific Force. In the summer of 1944, he was posted to Washington as the Deputy Chief of Naval Operations (Air). (US Naval Historical Center)

Captain Frederick Sherman in 1938 before assuming command of the carrier *Lexington*. His career was not affected by the loss of his ship at the Coral Sea, and he went on to gain flag rank and to command carrier task forces later in the war. (US Naval Historical Center)

During the actual carrier battle phase, Fletcher gave tactical control of the carrier task force over to **Rear Admiral Aubrey Fitch**. At the time, Fitch commanded one of the two carrier divisions in the Pacific Fleet. (The other was commanded by the US Navy's senior naval aviator, Vice Admiral William F. Halsey.) Fitch was junior to Fletcher but had considerable carrier experience. He qualified as a pilot in 1930 at age 47, and thus became known as a "Johnny Come Lately" to officers who had spent their entire career as aviators. After becoming an aviator, he commanded two carriers, two naval air stations and a patrol wing. He was considered to be a very competent naval officer.

The captains of the two American carriers at Coral Sea were both naval aviators, as were all carrier skippers per US Navy regulation. The captain of *Yorktown* was **Elliott Buckmaster**. Buckmaster was known for his excellent seamanship and his willingness to let his aviators experiment. *Yorktown*'s air group had become one of the best in the fleet. **Captain Frederick "Ted" Sherman** had been commanding officer of *Lexington* for two years and had worked the ship into a high state of efficiency. He was one of the first US naval officers to realize the value of concentrating multiple carriers into a single task force and his thoughts were used during the Coral Sea battle even though it was against prevailing US Navy doctrine of the day. Later in the war he would become an outstanding leader of carrier task forces.

# OPPOSING FLEETS

## THE IJN CARRIER FORCE

In early 1942, the IJN's carrier force was at its zenith. Since the start of the war, no carriers had been lost and losses of carrier aircraft had been relatively light. The Kido Butai had accomplished every mission it had been assigned and had smashed all Allied opposition before it. However, it had yet to meet the US Navy's carrier force. In May 1942, the IJN's carrier force held both a numerical and qualitative edge over its American counterpart. Six fleet carriers, *Akagi*, *Kaga*, the two ships of the *Soryu* class and the two units of the *Shokaku* class, remained at the center of Japanese naval air power. The light carriers *Hosho*, *Ryujo* and the two units of the *Shoho* class supported the fleet carriers. One escort carrier, *Taiyo*, was also in service. Adding to the numerical advantage of the IJN was the May 1942 completion of the converted carrier *Junyo*, capable of carrying some 50 aircraft. Had this force remained massed as it had been during the first part of the war, it would have retained a numerical edge in any battle with the US Navy's carrier force. However, for the Coral Sea operation only three carriers would be committed.

*Hiryu*, shown here on sea trials in 1939, was the design basis for the larger and more successful *Shokaku* class. *Hiryu* and her sister ship *Soryu* formed Carrier Division 2 of the Kido Butai and were very active during the first part of the war. Neither ship was present at the Coral Sea, but both were committed to the Midway operation where they were sunk by American carrier air attack. (US Naval Historical Center)

### *The Shokaku class*

The heart of the MO Operation was the two ships of the *Shokaku* class, which made up the Kido Butai's Carrier Division 5. These ships were designed free of any naval treaty restrictions to specifications that called for a ship capable of operating a large air group while possessing high speed, good

protection and a large radius of action. The result was the epitome of Japanese carrier design and the most powerful and best-balanced carrier design in the Pacific until the advent of the US Navy's *Essex* class in 1943. The *Shokaku* was laid down in December 1937 and *Zuikaku* in May 1938 and both were barely completed and placed in service in time for the Pearl Harbor operation. The basis of the design was that of the preceding *Hiryu* class but with an additional 100ft in length and an approximate 8,500 extra tons of displacement. In spite of this increased size, the ships retained a very high speed owing to the fitting of the most powerful machinery ever on an IJN ship and a new bulbous bow that reduced underwater drag. Two hangars were provided and three elevators were installed to handle the large air group. A small island was placed forward on the starboard side.

In addition to their superb offensive capability, the *Shokakus* also carried a heavy defensive armament with eight Type 89 twin 5in. guns fitted in pairs, each with its own fire-control director. When commissioned, each ship also carried 12 25mm Type 96 triple mounts.

| HIJMS *Shokaku* and *Zuikaku* | |
|---|---|
| Displacement: 26,675 tons | Aircraft capacity: 84 (72 operational) |
| Dimensions: length 845ft; beam 85ft; draft 29ft | Radius: 9,700 miles |
| Maximum speed: 34 knots | Crew: 1,800 |

## The Shoho class

*Shoho* was originally designed as a high-speed oiler, but was completed as a submarine tender. Her real purpose was to provide a ready-made basis for conversion into a light carrier. As war loomed, conversion of the *Shoho* began in January 1941 and was completed one year later. When *Shoho* joined the fleet with her sister ship *Zuiho*, they were the most successful of the Japanese light carrier conversions. The simple conversion required that the original diesel engines be removed and replaced by destroyer turbines. The flight deck was fitted over the existing structure and two elevators served a single hangar deck. No island was fitted with navigation being accomplished from a position forward of the hangar. When completed, the *Shoho* possessed adequate speed and a useful air group. However, the ship possessed no protection.

A fine view of *Shoho* on December 20, 1941. Note the lack of an island. Navigation was accomplished from a small bridge located under the forward part of the flight deck. (Yamato Museum)

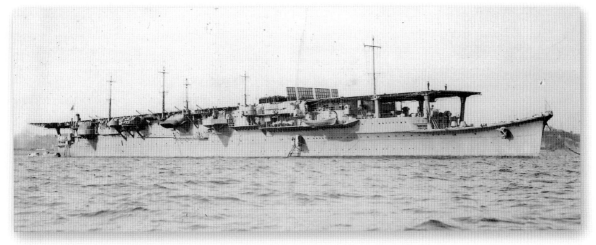

A beam shot of *Shoho* showing the hull lines of her former identify as a submarine tender. The two starboard side dual 5in. guns can be made out as can the two triple 25mm mounts aft of the downward canted exhaust stack. (Yamato Museum)

Defensive armament included four Type 89 twin 5in. mounts. The short-range anti-aircraft fit originally consisted of an inadequate four triple 25mm mounts.

**HIJMS *Shoho***

| | |
|---|---|
| Displacement: 11,262 tons | Aircraft capacity: 30 (27 operational) |
| Dimensions: length 712ft; beam 59ft; draft 22ft | Radius: 9,236 miles |
| Maximum speed: 28 knots | Crew: 785 |

## IJN *carrier air defense*

Unlike on American carriers, no Japanese carrier began the war fitted with radar. This situation persisted until after the battle of Midway. This made the task of controlling defending fighters very difficult. In the early-war period, half of the 18-aircraft fighter squadron was dedicated for defense. With no radar, air defense was accomplished by conducting standing patrols. However, only a few aircraft (usually a section of three) would be airborne at any time with the remaining aircraft standing by to be scrambled if adequate warning was gained. Adding further difficulty to the fighter defense problem was the inferior quality of Japanese aircraft radios that made it virtually impossible to control aircraft already airborne.

Overall, the effectiveness of the IJN's shipboard air defenses was inadequate throughout 1942, and this situation never really changed for the remainder of the war. Because Japanese shipboard anti-aircraft gunnery was unsuccessful in defending carriers from American air attack, the primary defense against air attack was mounted by fighters or by the ability of a carrier's captain to maneuver skillfully under attack. When exposed to air attack, Japanese carrier escorts maneuvered independently to give the carrier maximum room for maneuver. In contrast, American carrier escorts also gave the carrier room for radical maneuvers, but were still expected to stay close enough to the carrier to provide anti-aircraft support

Japanese anti-aircraft weaponry and fire control did not compare favorably to that of the US Navy in early 1942. The standard 5in. anti-aircraft weapon, the Type 89/40 was a respectable weapon, but its Type 94 fire-control director had difficulty tracking fast targets. Japanese 5in. gun crews were trained differently from their American counterparts. Unlike American crews, who practiced aimed fire, the Japanese crews were trained to use barrage fire. This may have been suitable against horizontal bombers forced to maintain a predictable course and speed, but it was ineffectual against more maneuverable carrier-based torpedo and dive-bombers. Since the Japanese never developed an effective intermediate-range, air-defense weapon during the war, the Type 96 25mm gun served in the intermediate and short-range roles. This weapon had many faults and even the Japanese recognized that it could not handle high-speed targets because it could not be trained or elevated fast enough by either hand or power and its sights were inadequate for high-speed targets. It also demonstrated excessive vibration and muzzle blast, and its magazines were too small to maintain high rates of fire. To add to the IJN's troubles, even when the Type 96 managed to hit its target, its small weight of shell (0.6 pounds) was most often ineffective against the rugged American Dauntless dive-bomber. The Type 96 was first introduced as a double mount and in 1941 a triple mount was introduced. Overall, Japanese anti-aircraft gunnery was only a minor factor during the battle of the Coral Sea.

## IJN carrier air groups

Even before the war, the primary mission of Japanese carriers was to sink their American counterparts. The events of the first few months of the war had only reinforced the necessity of gaining air superiority by eliminating the enemy's carriers. Like the US Navy, the Japanese viewed their own carriers as

A strike preparing to launch from the carrier *Shokaku*. This shot was taken during the battle of Santa Cruz in October 1942, but it shows a typical deck spot for a strike launch. The most forward aircraft are A6M2 Type 0 carrier fighters; further aft are D3A1 Type 99 carrier bombers. (US Naval Historical Center)

vulnerable to attack. Like every other component of the IJN, Japanese carriers were designed and trained for offensive warfare. In the case of carrier combat, the essential precondition for victory was to find the enemy's carriers first and launch overwhelming strikes as quickly as possible. Ideally, this would be done beyond the range at which the enemy could retaliate, explaining the great Japanese emphasis on large carrier air groups composed of aircraft uniformly lighter than their opponents, thus giving them greater range.

One important advantage exercised by the Japanese at the start of the war was their ability to mass carrier air power. In April 1941, the Japanese brought all their fleet carriers into a single formation, the First Air Fleet. The Kido Butai (literally "mobile force" but better given as "striking force") was the operational component of the First Air Fleet. Three carrier divisions made up the Kido Butai, including the Fifth with the newly completed *Shokaku* and *Zuikaku*. Unlike in the US Navy where the carrier division served only in an administrative capacity, the carrier divisions of the Kido Butai were operational entities. The two carriers of Carrier Division 5 fought as a single unit where squadrons of each carrier routinely trained and fought together. Typically, when multiple carrier operations were being conducted, the entire strike would be commanded by one of the carrier group commanders, who would direct the operations of the entire strike. Usually, the strike was accompanied by an escort of six to nine fighters from each carrier. Throughout 1942, including at the Coral Sea, the IJN was able to integrate operations from different carriers far better than the US Navy and routinely achieved a higher level of coordination.

Each Japanese carrier had its own air group. This air group was named after its parent ship and was permanently assigned to the ship. The aviators of the air group as well as all of the personnel required to support the aircraft were assigned to the ship's company.

*Shokaku*-class carriers had air groups made up of three different types of flying units. These included fighter, carrier bomber (dive-bombers) and carrier attack (torpedo bomber) squadrons. Each of these squadron equivalents also retained the name of their parent carrier. At the start of the war, *Shokaku*-class carriers embarked 72 aircraft broken down into one 18-aircraft fighter squadron and two 27-aircraft carrier bomber and carrier attack units. Even with relatively light aircraft losses, by May 1942 the IJN was unable to provide the two ships of Carrier Division 5 with any more than approximately 63 aircraft. The fighter units on *Shokaku* and *Zuikaku* were up to strength, but the attack squadrons for both carriers were some 25 percent under strength. As a light carrier, *Shoho* embarked only two types of squadrons, fighter and carrier attack. The fact that even light aircraft losses were already taxing the IJN's capability to provide replacements was again demonstrated by *Shoho*'s May 1942 air group. Her fighter squadron possessed only 12 aircraft, and of these four were the recently replaced A5M Type 96 fighters. *Shoho*'s carrier attack unit included only six aircraft. Altogether, *Shoho* embarked only 18 of her capacity of 27 aircraft.

Japanese carrier aircraft were designed for maximum range. This gave them an important edge over their American counterparts, but the penalty for this was reduced protection. The most dramatic example was the standard IJN carrier fighter, the A6M Type 0 (given the codename "Zero" by the Allies). Design specifications for this fighter were issued in 1937. The first variant, the A6M1, took to the air in April 1939. The A6M1 proved to be underpowered; with the provision of a larger 950hp engine, the A6M2

was born. In its day, the Type 0 fighter became a legend. While it was an inspired design that possessed exceptional maneuverability, great climb and acceleration, a relatively strong armament and unparalleled range for a fighter, it was not invincible. The Type 0 fighter's performance was achieved only by lightening the airframe as much as possible. This meant that the aircraft possessed almost no armor and the pilot and fuel tanks were vulnerable to damage from even small-caliber weapons.

**Specifications for Mitsubishi A6M2 Type 0 carrier fighter plane Model 21**

Crew: one
Armament: two 7.7mm machine guns and two 20mm cannon
Maximum speed: 336mph at 19,685ft
Range: 1,160 miles

Owing to the shortage of aircraft, *Shoho*'s fighter unit possessed a mixed unit of A6M and A5M fighters. The A5M (or "Claude" to Allied intelligence) was first delivered into fleet service in 1937 and was clearly outmoded in 1942 with its open cockpit, inferior speed and light armament.

**Specifications for Mitsubishi A5M4 Type 96 carrier fighter plane Model 34**

Crew: one
Armament: two 7.7mm machine guns
Maximum speed: 270mph at 9,845ft
Range: 746 miles

The Aichi D3A1 Type 99 Carrier Bomber was the IJN's standard shipborne dive-bomber for the first half of the war. The markings of this Type 99 show it to be from *Zuikaku*. (*Ships of the World* Magazine)

The IJN called its dive-bombers "carrier bombers." The standard carrier bomber at the start of the war was the D3A1 Type 99 carrier bomber. It was given the codename "Val" by the Allies. The provision of fixed landing gear gave the aircraft a dated appearance, but the Type 99 was a very effective dive-bomber designed to maintain a stable dive of up to 80 degrees to attain maximum accuracy. Overall, the Type 99 was not the equal of the American SBD Dauntless. It did not carry self-sealing fuel tanks, it lacked the ruggedness of the US dive-bomber, and it could not carry as heavy a payload as the Dauntless.

Close-up shot of the cockpit and the Type 91 air-launched torpedo carried aboard a Type 97 carrier attack plane. The combination of this relatively fast torpedo plane and an excellent torpedo provided the IJN with a superb ship-killing capability. (US Naval Historical Center)

Crew: two

Armament: one 551-pound centerline bomb; two 132-pound bombs under the wings; two forward-firing 7.7mm and one rear-firing 7.7mm machine gun

Maximum speed: 240mph at 9,845ft

Range: 915 miles

Rounding out the Japanese air groups were what the IJN called "carrier attack planes." This aircraft possessed the capability to operate as a torpedo bomber or a horizontal bomber, depending on the target. By 1942, the standard carrier attack plane was the B5N2 Type 97 carrier attack plane (codenamed "Kate" by the Allies). The Type 97 was greatly superior to the standard US Navy torpedo bomber of early 1942 in key areas such as speed, climb and range. Increasing the edge enjoyed by the Japanese was the much greater reliability of Japanese torpedoes over their American counterparts. The rugged nature of Japanese torpedoes allowed them to be dropped from higher altitudes and at higher speeds. However, the Type 97 did possess the same weakness as other Japanese carrier aircraft with range and performance being achieved at the expense of protection.

Crew: three

Armament : one 1,764-pound torpedo or 1,764 pounds of bombs; one flexible rear-firing 7.7mm machine gun

Maximum speed: 235mph at 11,810ft

Range: 608 miles

# THE US NAVY CARRIER FORCE

The Pacific Fleet's carrier force was untouched in the Pearl Harbor attack. *Enterprise* and *Lexington* were both in the area of Pearl Harbor, but very fortunately for the US Navy, were not actually in the harbor on December 7. Numerically, the US Navy had a fleet carrier force equal to the Japanese in 1942, but in terms of employment, aircraft capabilities and personnel training,

*Ranger* was the US Navy's first attempt to design a fleet carrier from the keel up. Her design was considered a failure, but several of the features introduced were employed on the more successful *Yorktown* class. *Ranger* did not see combat action in the Pacific. (US Naval Historical Center)

Lexington in February 1933 pictured off the Hawaiian Islands. The ship's battlecruiser lineage and the large stack aft of the small bridge are evident. The US Navy's emphasis on embarking a large air group can be seen by the large numbers of aircraft spotted forward and aft on the flight deck. (US Naval Historical Center)

the two opposing carrier forces were very different. The US Navy had been developing carrier aviation since the 1920s. By 1942, it was a large force with seven fleet carriers built around two main classes. Additionally, there were two unique carriers, *Ranger* and *Wasp*. Both were seen as inferior designs; *Ranger* was never committed to combat duty in the Pacific and *Wasp* arrived in the Pacific later in 1942 and was quickly sunk.

## Lexington class

Entering service in 1928, the two ships of this class, *Lexington* and *Saratoga*, were the first true US Navy fleet carriers. As carriers converted from battlecruisers, they were large, displacing 36,000 tons. Their most salient feature was the huge smokestack on the starboard side located just behind the separate island. The island was small and contained gunnery and aircraft control as well as navigation facilities. Given their battlecruiser ancestry, both were very fast, but since they were the longest ships in the world at the time, they were not very maneuverable and took a while to answer the helm. The *Lexington* was the more modern of the two sisters since before the war she had had her bow widened expanding the size of the flight deck. In 1940, a CXAM air search radar was installed on the forward part of *Lexington*'s stack.

Lexington pictured prior to the war in October 1941. The 8in. gun mounts fitted fore and aft of the island and stack, originally fitted for protection against cruiser attack, remain aboard and would not be removed until April 1942. Her prewar air group includes Brewster F2A Buffalo fighters spotted forward, as well as Dauntless dive-bombers and Devastator torpedo aircraft spotted amidships and aft. The Devastators can be distinguished by their folding wings. (US Naval Historical Center)

For anti-aircraft protection, 12 single 5in./25 gun mounts were positioned on sponsons on the corners of the flight deck. To counter the threat of dive-bombing, both ships carried a large battery of automatic weapons. Beginning in 1940, 1.1in. quadruple machine-cannons were installed. Five of these weapons were fitted, reducing the number of single .50-cal. machine guns to 28. The outbreak of war saw further augmentation of the anti aircraft battery. *Lexington* had her 8in. guns removed in April 1942. At Coral Sea, she mounted a total of 12 quadruple 1.1in. mounts, 32 20mm guns and 28 machine guns.

**USS *Lexington***

| | |
|---|---|
| Displacement: 36,000 tons | Aircraft capacity: 90 |
| Dimensions: length 888ft; beam 105ft; draft 32ft | Radius: 6,960 miles |
| Maximum speed: 34kts | Crew: 2,122 (pre-war) |

## *Yorktown class*

The three ships of the *Yorktown* class were the first truly modern US Navy fleet carriers and proved so successful they formed the basis for the even more successful *Essex* design. Generally an improved *Ranger* design, these 20,000-ton ships were large enough to permit the incorporation of protection against torpedo attack. A four-inch side armor belt was fitted over the machinery spaces, magazines and gasoline storage tanks. Vertical protection was limited to 1.5in. of armor over the machinery spaces. The main deck was the hangar deck with the unarmored flight deck being built of light steel. The primary design focus of the class was to provide adequate space to operate a large air group. To support the air group quickly and efficiently, three deck elevators were fitted to move aircraft between the hangar and flight decks and the large hangar deck was serviced by large roller curtains which could be opened to allow aircraft to warm up prior to launch, thus speeding flight operations. The large island was fitted with spaces for conning and navigation, control of aircraft and fire control for defensive weapons.

The *Yorktown* class also received a heavy defensive battery to counter enemy air attack. This class was among the first US Navy ships equipped with the new 5in./38 dual-purpose guns, which proved to be the best long-range anti-aircraft weapon of the war in any navy. The eight 5in./38 guns

Yorktown pictured in 1937 just after commissioning. She was the lead ship in the US Navy's first class of modern carriers. Besides rendering outstanding wartime service, the *Yorktown* class provided the design basis for the even more successful *Essex* class. (US Naval Historical Center)

were controlled by a pair of Mark 33 directors mounted on the island. For intermediate and close-in protection, four 1.1in. quadruple mounts were placed fore and aft of the island and a total of 24 .50-cal. machine guns were fitted on the gallery deck. Before the battle of the Coral Sea, *Yorktown* had received 20mm single mounts in place of the ineffective .50-cal. weapons. Another important improvement was the addition of radar. *Yorktown* was one of the ships to receive one of the first six CXAM sets in October 1940. CXAM was an air search radar that used a very large mattress-like antenna. Increases in power, and therefore detection ranges, led to the introduction of the CXAM-1 radar. With an accuracy of 200yds, it was capable of detecting a large aircraft or aircraft formation flying at 10,000 feet at 70 nautical miles or a small aircraft at 50 nautical miles.

**USS *Yorktown***

Displacement: 19,576 tons

Dimensions: length 810ft; beam 110ft; draft 25ft

Maximum speed: 33kts

Aircraft capacity: 81

Radius: 11,200 miles at 15 knots

Crew (1941): 227 Officers, 1,990 enlisted personnel (including air group)

## US carrier air defense

Prior to the war, the US Navy viewed its aircraft carriers as vulnerable, reflecting the belief that carriers could not withstand significant damage. This notion drove US carrier designers to achieve maximum offensive potential in the hopes that a quick strike would remove the enemy carrier threat. This also drove prewar carrier doctrine that carriers should be separated in the hope that they would avoid simultaneous detection and destruction. By April 1942, with the benefit of limited war experience, carrier air defense remained a weakness. However, the US Navy had the great advantage of possessing radar. This carried the promise that an effective fleet air defense could be mounted as now approaching enemy aircraft could be detected well beyond visual range and defending fighters could be sent out to intercept the intruders at a distance from friendly carriers. However, in early 1942, this was only a theoretical advantage as radar fighter direction was in its early stages. Communication problems and the inability of early radar to give reliable altitudes, combined with a general lack of experience, would greatly complicate fighter direction.

Typically, half of a carrier's fighters would be retained for fleet air defense. These were used to mount standing combat air patrols (CAP) of two to three hours' duration during daylight hours above the carrier. The remaining fighters would be fueled and armed on deck ready for launch to augment the existing patrols. Some carriers (including *Yorktown* and *Lexington)* had the doctrine of augmenting their CAP with Dauntless dive-bombers assigned to anti-torpedo plane patrol. These were conducted at low altitudes in the immediate area of the home carrier in an effort to augment defenses against low-flying and relatively slow torpedo planes.

Augmenting the defensive efforts of the carrier's air group were the anti-aircraft guns aboard the carrier and its escorts. The American long-range air defense gun during 1942 was the 5in. dual-purpose gun. The unrivaled 5in./38 gun was mounted aboard *Yorktown* and the escorting destroyers. It was an accurate gun and, most importantly for anti-aircraft use, had a high rate of fire. A well-drilled crew could get off 20 rounds per minute out

to a maximum of 18,200yds. The older 5in./25 gun aboard *Lexington* and the escorting cruisers was still a capable weapon, but possessed a shorter range of 14,500yds. These weapons used fire-control directors or local control to engage individual targets or were used to place a barrage in front of attacking enemy aircraft.

Intermediate and short-range anti-aircraft protection was provided by a mix of guns. During early 1942, intermediate defense was provided by the 1.1in. machine cannon. This was a four-barreled, water-cooled system that could deliver a rate of fire of 140 rounds per minute per barrel. However, in service

The heavy cruiser *Portland* saw extensive service as a carrier escort in the early parts of the war. She would be assigned to screen *Yorktown* at both the Coral Sea and Midway. (US Naval Historical Center)

The standard 5in. gun aboard all US heavy cruisers at the Coral Sea was the 5in./25 gun. This is the Number 3 mount aboard heavy cruiser *Astoria*. (US Naval Historical Center)

The port side forward battery of 20mm Oerlikon guns on *Yorktown*. Early in the war, the 20mm proliferated throughout the fleet as a replacement for the ineffective .50-cal. machine gun. The 20mm could be deployed anywhere with a clear arc of fire by simply bolting the weapon to the deck. Though an improvement over the .50-cal. machine gun, it still lacked the range to engage enemy aircraft before they had an opportunity to drop their weapons. (US Naval Historical Center)

it proved disappointing owing to continual jamming problems. Last-ditch air defense was provided by the remaining .50-cal. machine guns and the 20mm Oerlikon gun, which was being mounted in increasing numbers aboard American carriers and other ships throughout 1942. Since the weapon was lightweight and required no external power source, it could be mounted anywhere with a clear arc of fire. Aiming was performed through a ring site and fire spotted through the use of tracers. However, with an effective range of 2,000yds or less, these short-ranged weapons had two critical disadvantages. In general, only the ship being attacked could use them and when a target was engaged, it had likely already dropped its weapon. Gunnery against aerial targets was given a high priority and American gunners incessantly trained with their weapons. However, by May 1942 American anti-aircraft gunnery was limited to inflicting relatively minor losses on attacking Japanese aircraft.

### American air groups

Early 1942 American carrier strike doctrine was less mature than that practiced by the IJN. Typically, in the morning, a number of dive-bombers would be launched to perform reconnaissance. If a target was located, a strike was launched as soon as possible with every available dive-bomber and torpedo plane. The fighter squadron was usually divided with half providing strike escort and the other half providing CAP. The problem with US Navy strike doctrine was that it remained focused on the operations of a single air group from a single carrier. While the Japanese had made the mental leap to mass all their fleet carriers into a single unit and could operate aircraft from multiple carriers as a single entity in combat, the US Navy maintained the practice of forming a task force around a single carrier which in turn meant that strikes were conducted by single air groups. Ideally, the dive-bombers and torpedo bombers would conduct a coordinated strike against a high-value target (like an enemy carrier). By attacking together, they would split the target's defenses which was an important factor given the potential vulnerability of the torpedo planes. However, serious problems existed in coordinating strikes even within air groups and coordinating strikes from different carriers was virtually impossible.

Complicating the task of American carriers was the fact that the ranges of their aircraft were inferior to that of the Japanese. The scout squadrons were usually charged to conduct scouting missions. These were conducted in the morning and afternoon out to a usual range of 150–200 miles. In this role they retained a 500-pound bomb to strike anything they found. Strike missions were conducted by both the scout and dive-bomber squadrons. In the strike role, the Dauntless dive-bomber had a doctrinal strike radius of 225 miles with a 500-pound bomb and 175 miles with a full 1,000-pound bomb load. Torpedo bombers were limited to a range of 150 miles with a full torpedo load. The strike range of escorting fighters was limited to that of the torpedo bombers since no auxiliary fuel tanks were used at this point of the war.

US Navy 1942 air groups were composed of four squadrons. The fighter squadron was equipped with 18 F4F Wildcat fighters. Two squadrons were equipped with the Douglas SBD-2/3 Dauntless dive-bomber. One squadron was named a scouting squadron and the second a bombing squadron, though in practice both squadrons performed virtually identically. Dive-bombing squadrons possessed between 16–21 aircraft. The air group commander usually was assigned his own dive-bomber. The torpedo squadron was assigned 12–18 TBD Devastator aircraft. Each TBD could carry a single torpedo or carry bombs and act as horizontal bombers. In the early war period, US Navy carriers each had a permanently assigned air group. Each of the assigned squadrons carried the hull number of the ship it was assigned to. For example, *Lexington's* fighter squadron was numbered VF-2, her dive-bombers VB-2, her scout bombers VS-2 and her torpedo squadron VT-2.

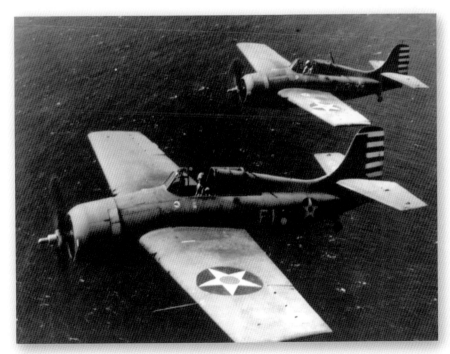

Grumman F4F-3A Wildcats of VF-3 pictured in April 1942. Both of the aircraft pictured were later assigned to VF-2 during the battle of the Coral Sea and were lost. The Wildcat's first meeting with the Japanese A6M Type 0 carrier fighter at the Coral Sea showed the American fighter to be outclassed, but American pilots were able to overcome the Wildcat's weaknesses with better tactics. (US Naval Historical Center)

Dauntless dive-bombers of *Yorktown's* Bombing Squadron Five shown on deck in April 1942. The Dauntless dive-bomber was the primary offensive weapon of US Navy carrier air groups, as events during the battle of the Coral Sea would demonstrate. (US Naval Historical Center)

The standard US Navy ship-borne fighter during 1942 was the F4F "Wildcat." This was a modern design first flown in 1937. The version in service during Coral Sea was the F4F-4. The F4F-4 was introduced into the Pacific Fleet in April 1942 and featured several important differences including folding wings, six guns (*vice* four on the F4F-3) and factory-installed armor and self-sealing fuel tanks. All of these changes affected the aircraft's climb and maneuverability. The Wildcat was no match for the Japanese "Zero" carrier-based fighter, but Wildcat pilots compensated for inferior aircraft with excellent gunnery skills against airborne targets and superior tactics.

**Specifications for Grumman F4F-4 Wildcat carrier fighter**

Crew: one
Armament: six wing-mounted .50-cal. machine guns
Maximum speed: 318mph at 19,400ft
Combat radius: 175 miles

The backbone of US carrier air groups was its two dive-bomber squadrons equipped with the Douglas SBD "Dauntless" dive-bomber. During a time when American carrier torpedo aircraft lacked an effective torpedo, the Dauntless constituted the striking power of the US Navy's carrier air groups. It was accepted into service in 1939. By 1942, the SDB-3 was the primary model in service, and it mounted a dual machine gun for the rear gunner and carried improved armor and self-sealing fuel tanks. The Dauntless was a rugged aircraft able to absorb considerable combat damage, but it was most famous for being a stable and accurate bombing platform. Its only drawbacks were a mediocre top speed and non-folding wings that made movement and storage on carrier hangar and flight decks more difficult.

**Specifications for Douglas SDB-3 Dauntless carrier dive-bomber**

Crew: two

Armament: 1,600 pounds of bombs with another 650 pounds under wings; two cowl-mounted .50-cal. machine guns and two flexible .30-cal. rear-mounted machine guns

Maximum speed: 255mph at 14,000ft

Combat radius: 225 miles, depending on bomb load

Rounding out American carrier air groups was the TBD "Devastator." This aircraft dated back to 1937, and while it constituted a major advancement for its day, by 1941 it was clearly obsolescent. The primary shortcoming of the Devastator was its slow speed and short combat radius. To top things off, the US Navy's aerial torpedo, the Mark XIII, was notoriously unreliable and could not be dropped above 100mph or above 120 feet, which made the Devastator exceedingly vulnerable.

**Specifications for Douglas TBD-1 Devastator torpedo bomber**

Crew: three

Armament: one torpedo or 1,000 pounds of bombs; one .30- or .50-cal. nose-mounted machine gun and one .30-cal. flexible rear-mounted machine gun

Maximum speed: 206mph at 8,000ft

Combat Radius: 150 miles with ordnance

## Intelligence

Perhaps the most important American advantage in the naval battles of early 1942 was in the arena of operational intelligence. In addition to the traditional means of traffic analysis of IJN radio messages (which provided insights into subordination, order of battle and operational tempo), the Americans had an even more valuable source of radio intelligence. The Americans had been making steady progress in cracking the IJN code in use since the start of the war. This code, known to the Americans as JN-25B, employed a double, and later a triple cipher system. By March 1942, the Americans had made enough progress on breaking the internals of the system to start piecing together parts of messages. By April, real advances had been made against JN-25B, which allowed up to 85 percent of some signals to be read. This effort was made possible by the delay in a scheduled IJN code change that was pushed back from April 1 to May 1, and finally June 1. The importance of this breakthrough was demonstrated when, on April 9, Nimitz received the first indication by signals intelligence that a Japanese move into the South Pacific was likely. Eventually, signals intelligence would discern the target of the Japanese operation and provide a very close idea of the forces to be committed to it. However, despite many claims to the contrary, radio intelligence was not a decisive factor during the 1942 battles of the Coral Sea and Midway. However, for the outnumbered US Navy, it was an invaluable tool since it allowed Nimitz to position his forces with the best likelihood for success.

# ORDERS OF BATTLE

## IMPERIAL JAPANESE NAVY
### TASK FORCE MO

(Vice Admiral Inoue Shigeyoshi (Commander, 4th Fleet) aboard light cruiser *Kashima* in Rabaul)

**MO Carrier Striking Force** (Vice Admiral Takagi Takeo) *

Carrier Division 5 (Rear Admiral Hara Tadaichi)

Carrier *Shokaku* (Captain Jojima Takaji)

| *Shokaku* Air Group (Lieutenant-Commander Takahashi Kakuichi) | one D3A1 |
|---|---|
| *Shokaku* Carrier Fighter Unit | 18 A6M2 |
| *Shokaku* Carrier Bomber Unit | 20 D3A1 |
| *Shokaku* Carrier Attack Unit | 19 B5N2 |
| Total | 58 (56 operational) |

(plus another three A6M2 for Tainan Air Group in Rabaul)

Carrier *Zuikaku* (Captain Yokogawa Ichihei)

| *Zuikaku* Air Group (Lieutenant-Commander Shimazaki Shigekazu) | one B5N2* |
|---|---|
| *Zuikaku* Carrier Fighter Unit | 20 A6M2 |
| *Zuikaku* Carrier Bomber Unit | 22 D3A1 |
| *Zuikaku* Carrier Attack Unit | 20 B5N2 |
| Total | 63 (53 operational) |

(plus another five A6M2 for Tainan Air Group in Rabaul)

Cruiser Division 5

Heavy cruisers *Myoko*, *Haguro*

Destroyer Division 7

Destroyers *Ushio*, *Akebono*

Destroyer Division 27

Destroyers *Ariake*, *Yugure*, *Shiratsuyu*, *Shigure*

Oiler Toho Maru

**MO Main Force** (Rear Admiral Goto Aritomo) *

Light carrier *Shoho* (Captain Izawa Ishinosuke)

| *Shoho* Air Group (Lieutenant Notomi Kenjiro)* | |
|---|---|
| *Shoho* Carrier Fighter Unit | eight A6M2, four A5M2 |
| *Shoho* Carrier Attack Unit | six B5N2 |
| Total | 18 (18 operational) |

Cruiser Division 6

Heavy cruisers *Aoba*, *Kako*, *Kinugasa*, *Furutaka*

Destroyer *Sazanami* (from Destroyer Division 7)

**MO Invasion Force** (Rear Admiral Kajioka Sadamichi)

Destroyer Flotilla 6

Light cruiser *Yubari*

Destroyer Squadron 29

Destroyers *Oite*, *Asanagi*

Destroyer Squadron 30

Destroyers *Mutsuki*, *Mochizuki*, *Yayoi*

Destroyer Squadron 23

Destroyer *Uzuki*

Minelayer *Tsugaru*

Fleet minesweeper Number 20

Navy transports: *Goyo Maru, Akihasan Maru, Shokai Maru, Chowa Maru, Mogamikawa Maru*

Ocean tug *Oshima*

Army transports: *Matsue Maru, Taifuku Maru, Mito Maru, China Maru, Nichibi Maru, Asakasan Maru* carrying bulk of 3rd Kure Special Naval landing Force, 10th Establishment Unit, (construction troops) and 144th Infantry Regiment (South Seas Detachment)

**Covering Force** (Rear Admiral Marumo Kuninori)

Cruiser Division 18

Light cruisers *Tatsuta, Tenryu*

Seaplane carrier *Kamikawa Maru* (with air group from *Kiyokawa Maru*)

5th Gunboat Squadron

Specially fitted gunboats *Nikkai Maru, Keijo Maru*

Transport *Shoei Maru* carrying elements of 3rd Kure Special Naval Landing Force

14th Minesweeper Flotilla

*Hagoromo Maru, Noshiro Maru Number 2* (from Tulagi Invasion Force May 3)

**Tulagi Invasion Force** (Rear Admiral Shima Kiyohide)

Minelayer *Okinoshima*

23rd Destroyer Squadron

Destroyers *Kikuzuki, Yuzuki*

14th Minesweeper Flotilla

*Tama Maru, Hagoromo Maru, Noshiro Maru Number 2* (moved to MO Covering Force May 3)

*Special Minesweeper Number 1, Special Minesweeper Number 2*

56th Submarine Chaser Squadron

Patrol boats *Tama Maru Number 8, Toshi Maru Number 3*

Transports *Azumayama Maru* and *Koei Maru* carrying elements of 3rd Kure Special Naval Landing Force and 7th Establishment Unit (construction troops)

**Supply units**

Oilers *Ishiro, Hoyo Maru*

**Raiding Force**

21st Submarine Squadron

Submarines *RO-33, RO-34*

**Land-based Air Force** **

25th Air Flotilla, 5th Air Attack Force (Rear Admiral Yamada Sadayoshi at Rabaul)

28 A6M2 fighters (18 operational)

11 A5M2 fighters (six operational)

28 G4M land-based bombers (17 operational)

26 G3M land-based bombers (25 operational)

16 H6K4 flying boats (12 operational)

Fighters based at Lae, New Guinea and Launai Airfield at Rabaul. Bombers based at Vunakanau Airfileld at Rabaul. Flying boats initially based at Rabaul; later moved to Shortland and Tulagi Islands

*Strengths shown for evening, May 6, 1942
**Strengths shown for May 1, 1942

# ALLIED FORCES

## TASK FORCE 17

(Rear Admiral Frank Jack Fletcher)

Carrier Group Task Group 17.5 (Rear Admiral Aubrey Fitch)

| | |
|---|---|
| *Lexington* (Captain Frederick Sherman) | |
| *Lexington* Air Group (Commander William Ault) | one SBD-3* |
| Fighting Two (VF-2) | 21 F4F-3 |
| Bombing Two (VB-2) | 18 SBD-2/3 |
| Scouting Two (VS-2) | 17 SBD-3 |
| Torpedo Two (VT-2) | 13 TBD-1 |
| Total | 70 (66 operational) |
| *Yorktown* (Captain Elliott Buckmaster) | |
| *Yorktown* Air Group (Lieutenant Commander Oscar Pederson)* | |
| Fighting Forty-two (VF-42) | 17 F4F-3 |
| Bombing Five (VB-5) | 18 SBD-3 |
| Scouting Five (VS-5) | 17 SBD-3 |
| Torpedo Five (VT-5) | 12 TBD-1 |
| Total | 64 (62 operational) |

Destroyer screen

Destroyers *Morris, Anderson, Hammann, Russell*

**Attack Group Task Group 17.2** (Rear Admiral Thomas Kinkaid)

Heavy cruisers *Minneapolis, New Orleans, Astoria, Chester, Portland*

Destroyers *Phelps, Dewey, Farragut*, (attached to TG-17.3, May 7), *Alywin, Monaghan*

**Support Group Task Group 17.3** (Rear Admiral J. G. Crace, Royal Navy)**

Cruisers HMAS *Australia*, HMAS *Hobart, Chicago*

Destroyers *Perkins, Walke*

**Fueling Group Task Group 17.6** (Captain John Phillips)

Oilers *Neosho, Tippecanoe*

Destroyers *Sims, Worden*

**Search Group Task Force 17.9** (Commander George DeBaun)

Seaplane Tender *Tangier* (located at Noumea) with 12 PBY-5 Catalina flying boats
from patrol squadrons VP-71, VP-72

**Task Force 42 Eastern Australia Submarine Group** (Rear Admiral Francis Rockwell)
(under Southwest Pacific Area command)

TG-42.1 in submarine tender *Griffin* located at Brisbane

Submarine Division 53

*S-42, S-43, S-44, S-45, S-46, S-47*

Submarine Division 201

*S-37, S-38, S-39, S-40, S-41*

Of these boats, only *S-38, S-42, S-44* and *S-47* were able to go to sea before the
battle began

**Allied Air Forces** (Lieutenant-General George Brett, United States Army)
under command of Southwest Pacific Area ***

Fighter groups

8th Pursuit Group; two squadrons at Port Moresby equipped with P-400 Airacobras.

Total strength of group approximately 100 aircraft (full strength)

35th Pursuit Group located at Mascot Airfield, Sydney, equipped with P-39.

Total strength of group approximately 100 aircraft (full strength)

49th Pursuit Group located at Port Darwin equipped with approximately 90 P-40

Bomber groups
    3rd Bombardment Group (Light) (located at Charters Towers)
        8th Light Squadron (19 assigned A-24 (USAAF version of SBD Dauntless))
        13th Light Squadron (assigned 19 former Dutch B-25)
        19th Light Squadron (assigned 14 A-20)
    22nd Bombardment Group (Medium) (Townsville)
        Full strength with 80 B-26 and 12 B-25
    19th Bombardment Group (Heavy) (Cloncurry)
        48 B-17

## Royal Australian Air Force
    11th and 12th Squadrons equipped with PBY Catalina; both at half-strength
        (total six aircraft). Stationed on Tulagi until May 2
    32nd General Reconnaissance Bomber Squadron equipped with Hudsons.
    75th Squadron equipped with P-40 and stationed at Port Moresby. Strength on
        April 30 was three operational aircraft.
    All four squadrons totaled 30 operational aircraft at start of battle


\* Aircraft strengths as of dawn May 7
\*\* This is the organization as of 0700 May 6, 1942. Previously, TF-17 was composed of *Yorktown*, heavy cruisers *Astoria, Chester* and *Portland* and the four destroyers assigned to TG-17.5. TF-11 included *Lexington*, heavy cruisers *New Orleans* and *Minneapolis* and the five destroyers assigned to TG-17.2. During the battle, TG-17.2 never operated as an independent entity. TG-17.3 was the renamed TF-44 from Southwest Pacific Area.
\*\*\* Aircraft strengths as of May 1

# OPPOSING PLANS

## THE JAPANESE PLAN: THE NAVAL GENERAL STAFF VS. THE COMBINED FLEET

The initial period of the Pacific War had gone according to the plans devised by the Imperial General Headquarters. The first operational stage outlined the need to occupy the Philippines, British Malaya, the Dutch East Indies, Burma and Rabaul. Following this, the second operational stage would expand Japan's strategic depth by adding eastern New Guinea, New Britain, the Aleutians, Midway, the Fijis, Samoa and "strategic points in the Australian area."

The Japanese commander in the South Pacific, Admiral Inoue, played a large role in shaping operations in the region. He succeeded in getting Rabaul added to the first operational stage when he pointed out that the main Japanese base in the Central Pacific at Truk was only just over 800 miles away. Once he had seized Rabaul, Inoue contended that its protection required seizing additional points to provide defensive depth. These included New Britain, eastern New Guinea (Lae and Salamaua) and Tulagi in the Solomons. Once these were occupied, the Japanese could set up a network of air bases to defeat Allied attacks. Accordingly, the Naval General Staff approved the seizure of Lae, Salamaua, Tulagi and Port Moresby on January 29, 1942. Port Moresby was especially important as it would eliminate the threat of American long-range bombing attacks on Rabaul while providing Japanese aircraft access to the Coral Sea and targets in northeastern Australia.

The heavy cruiser *Kinugasa* was very active in the first few months of the war participating in the Japanese operations at Wake Island, Rabaul and Lae–Salamaua. She was armed with six 8in. guns and eight 24in. torpedo tubes. (Yamato Museum)

*Kako*, shown in 1941, was one of four heavy cruisers assigned to the MO Main Body. The ship's two E7K2 Type 94 reconnaissance seaplanes are evident. Also shown is the ship's inadequate anti-aircraft armament of four single 4.7in. gun mounts and four twin 25mm guns. (Yamato Museum)

The first part of the second operational stage went smoothly when Lac and Salamaua were captured on March 8. However, the Japanese illusion of a continued run of unchallenged successes was shattered on March 10 when American carrier-based aircraft struck the Japanese invasion force. In addition to inflicting considerable losses on Inoue's small command, it stopped consideration of additional advances until Japanese forces in the region were reinforced to deal with potential future intervention by American carriers.

Therefore, the prospects for continued expansion in the South Pacific depended on the willingness of Yamamoto to contribute some of the Combined Fleet's carriers to the effort. This appeared doubtful from the start. While the Naval General Staff and the Navy Section of Imperial General Headquarters pondered how to get the Port Moresby operation going again, and even went as far as to study operations to seize New Caledonia, the Fijis and Samoa after the rescheduled Port Moresby operation, Yamamoto's gaze was firmly fixed on the Central Pacific. Here he thought he could arrange a decisive battle with what he considered as the American center of gravity – the carriers of the US Pacific Fleet. He preferred to put off any South Pacific expedition until his decisive clash at Midway could be finished. During the first week of April, the issue of future strategy was decided in Yamamoto's

*Kashima* served as Vice Admiral Inoue's flagship during the MO Operation in Rabaul. *Kashima* was one of three 5,890-ton training cruisers completed before the war. During the first part of the war, they were used as fleet flagships before the two surviving units were converted into anti-submarine ships in 1944. (Yamato Museum)

favor and his plan to attack Midway approved. However, in a move to placate the Naval General Staff, it was also agreed that the Kido Butai's Carrier Division 5 would be made available to support the Port Moresby operation before it was used in the Midway operation.

The attack on Port Moresby, codenamed the MO Operation, was divided into several phases. In the first phase, Rear Admiral Shima Kiyohide's Tulagi Invasion Force would advance down the Solomon Islands chain to protect the left flank of the operation and extend the range of Japanese air searches. The first objective was to move six flying boats and nine floatplanes from Rabaul to Shortland on April 28. On May 2, the short-ranged floatplanes would move to Thousand Ship Bay on the south end of Santa Isabel Island. This would support the seizure of Tulagi, which was scheduled to begin on May 3. Also supporting the attack on Tulagi was Goto's Main Force, principally the aircraft aboard *Shoho*. The Japanese expected lightly defended Tulagi to fall in a single day.

To Inoue, the threat of land-based aircraft was the greatest threat to the invasion of Port Moresby. The Allies would be able to base large numbers of aircraft in northeastern Australia, principally at the major bases at Townsville and Charters Towers. Complicating the issue for the Japanese, these bases were beyond the range of their land-based bombers at Rabaul. Despite the fact that a US carrier had struck Lae and Salamaua on March 10 (believed by the Japanese to have been the *Saratoga*), Inoue, among others, thought that no American carriers were still in the area.

Thus, at least initially, the primary job of the two fleet carriers assigned to the MO Striking Force was to take out the primary Allied air bases in Australia, not engage US carriers. To do this, and to minimize the chances of their early discovery, Takagi's carriers would conduct a wide sweep through the Coral Sea. The carriers would depart Truk and sail east of New Britain and the Solomon Islands. After the fall of Tulagi, the carriers would pass between San Cristobal and Espiritu Santo and enter the Coral Sea. Approaching from the east, not the north as the Allies would expect, the carriers would be in position on May 7 to execute a series of surprise air raids on Townsville.

The large 4,470-ton minelayer *Okinoshima* was the flagship of Rear Admiral Shima's Tulagi Invasion Force. After the seizure of Tulagi, Shima led an invasion force from Rabaul on May 10 with the goal of seizing the Ocean and Nauru islands. On May 11, *Okinoshima* was torpedoed and sunk by the American submarine *S-42*. The invasion attempt was called off when American carriers were spotted in the area on May 15. (Yamato Museum)

# The Southwest Pacific showing the Solomon Islands, eastern New Guinea, northwestern Australia and the Coral Sea

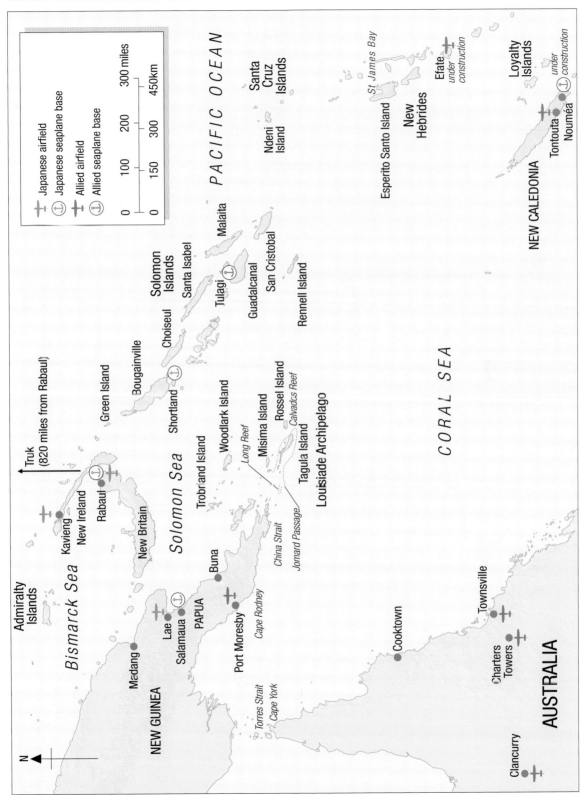

PACIFIC OCEAN

Japanese airfield
Japanese seaplane base
Allied airfield
Allied seaplane base

0    100    200    300 miles
0    150    300    450km

St James Bay

Efate
under construction

Santa Cruz Islands

Loyalty Islands

Ndeni Island

Esperito Santo Island

New Hebrides

Tontouta
Nouméa
under construction

Solomon Islands

Santa Isabel

Malaita

NEW CALEDONIA

Tulagi
Guadalcanal
San Cristobal

Rennell Island

Choiseul

Bougainville

Green Island

CORAL SEA

Shortland

Woodlark Island

Long Reef

Misima Island

Rossel Island

Calvados Reef

Trobriand Island

China Strait

Tagula Island

Louisiade Archipelago

Jomard Passage

Solomon Sea

Truk
(820 miles from Rabaul)

Kavieng
New Ireland

Rabaul

New Britain

Buna

Admiralty Islands

Bismarck Sea

Cape Rodney

Lae
Salamaua

PAPUA

Medang

Port Moresby

NEW GUINEA

Townsville

Cooktown

Torres Strait
Cape York

Charters Towers

AUSTRALIA

Clancurry

N

The heavy cruiser *Myoko* was the lead ship of a four-ship class. Two of these powerful ships were assigned as the primary screening units for the MO Carrier Striking Force. With ten 8in. guns and 16 24in. torpedoes, they were more heavily armed than any Allied cruiser in 1942. (Yamato Museum)

Supporting the movement of the carriers into the Coral Sea was the movement of the flying boats into Tulagi on May 4. These would provide direct reconnaissance support to the MO Carrier Striking Force. Indirect support was provided by the deployment of four submarines into a scouting line 450 miles southwest of Guadalcanal to intercept Allied naval forces moving north from Brisbane.

After their surprise attack on Townsville, the carriers would refuel and move into position in the center of the Coral Sea to intercept Allied naval forces that only then were expected to respond to the invasion. Additional air raids could be conducted on other air bases as required. Following the MO Operation, the carriers were scheduled to support forces moving down from the Marshall Islands to seize the Ocean and Nauru islands (the RY Operation). Following this, the carriers (including *Shoho*) would quickly return to Japan to be incorporated into the huge force being gathered for the MI Operation – the invasion of Midway.

The primary object of the whole operation was to get the invasion force to Port Moresby by the intended assault day of May 10. Doing so would be no easy feat since the slow-speed convoy had to transit over 1,000 miles from the Japanese base at Rabaul to its target. In the first leg, the invasion convoy would approach the Louisiade Archipelago and transit through the Jomard Passage. The second leg of the transit was from the Jomard Passage to Moresby – a distance of some 350 miles that would take two days. The invasion convoy would depart Rabaul on May 4. It would be covered by the Main Force, which would depart the Tulagi area and move north to join the invasion force. The Covering Force would set up a seaplane base at Deboyne Island in the central Louisiades to protect the convoy's transit and later set up another base at Cape Rodney east of Port Moresby. On May 10, the invasion would commence using units from the IJN's Kure 3rd Special Naval Landing Force and the South Seas Detachment from the Imperial Army built around the 144th Infantry Regiment.

The whole MO Operation featured a force of some 60 ships assigned to Vice Admiral Inoue Shigeyohi's South Seas Force. This included two large carriers, one light carrier, six heavy cruisers, three light cruisers and 15 destroyers. The balance of the force was composed of a variety of auxiliaries.

Altogether, some 250 aircraft were assigned to the operation (not including floatplanes) and of these, some 140 were aboard the three carriers. See pages 32–33 for the complete IJN order of battle for the MO Operation.

As was typical in Japanese operational planning, the MO Operation plan depended on close coordination of widely separated forces. Any delay in any aspect of the plan had the potential to throw the entire operation into jeopardy. This was amply demonstrated by the example of the MO Carrier Striking Force's mission of ferrying nine Type 0 fighters from Truk to Rabaul. The delay in executing this seemingly simple mission in turn delayed the arrival of the carriers into the Coral Sea, imperiling the entire operation. Even before its execution, the entire MO Operation plan had met severe resistance, not from the Americans, but from the admirals expected to execute it. Hara wanted no part of the planned air strikes against Australia, primarily because of his belief that there was no hope of achieving surprise. These concerns, and the growing suspicion on the part of the Japanese that American carriers could be present in the area prompted Inoue to authorize Takagi on April 29 to cancel the Townsville raid if surprise could not be achieved. The same day, Yamamoto weighed in and ordered that all strikes from the carriers against targets in Australia be cancelled and that the MO Carrier Striking Force was to be prepared instead to engage enemy carriers.

Thus the issue of dealing with Allied land-based air forces was left to the 25th Air Flotilla based at Rabaul. How this would be done was an open question since they could strike the airfields only at Port Moresby, leaving the bases in Australia untouched. The inability of the Japanese to provide air cover for the MO Invasion Force was the Achilles heel of the entire operation. Even if all three carriers had remained available to cover the convoy throughout the operation, protection against Allied land-based airpower would have been problematic. Since the burden of actual air defense to the convoy would have fallen to *Shoho* with her mere 12 fighters, had the battle developed favorably for the Japanese and the invasion convoy moved into the Coral Sea toward Port Moresby, the Japanese invasion could have been thwarted by land-based Allied aircraft without the need for a dramatic carrier battle.

The *Fubuki*-class destroyer *Sazanami* was assigned to the MO Main Body, primarily to act as a plane guard for the light carrier *Shoho*. Along with the two other *Fubuki*-class units assigned to the MO Carrier Striking Force, *Sazanami* had a powerful anti-ship armament of nine 24in. torpedo tubes capable of firing the powerful Type 93 torpedo and six 5in. guns, but possessed a negligible anti-aircraft armament in 1942. (Yamato Museum)

The most damning aspect of the plans for the MO Operation was its utter disregard for the actions of the enemy. By committing only a portion of the Kido Butai, Yamamoto not only jeopardized the success of the MO Operation, but exposed those units to defeat in detail. If those carriers were lost or damaged, they would be unable to participate in Yamamoto's decisive Midway operation. In fact, the two carriers of Carrier Division 5 constituted the decisive edge the IJN's carrier force held over the US Navy's carrier force. Thus, in essence, Yamamoto was making his decisive Midway operation hostage to the outcome of the subsidiary MO Operation.

## THE AMERICAN PLAN

King's first orders to the commander of the Pacific Fleet were to hold the key central Pacific positions at Hawaii and Midway, but also to protect the sea lines of communications from the US to Australia. This required the Hawaii to Samoa line to be secured as quickly as possible, followed by the line from Samoa to the Fiji Islands. King was determined that the "Germany first" strategy would not prevent him from local offensive operations. Japanese expansion into the South Pacific virtually ensured that King would get his way. The Japanese seizure of Rabaul on January 23 heightened fears that the Fijis or New Caledonia would be next. In response, King dispatched one carrier task force in January to the South Pacific (centered around *Lexington*), followed by another (centered on *Yorktown*) in mid-February.

In contrast to the elaborate Japanese plan, the US Navy's plan for the forthcoming battle was simple. On April 22, Nimitz sent his orders to Fletcher. He warned Fletcher about the impending Japanese offensive and gave him an idea of the size of the enemy force (three or four carriers). The heart of the directive was contained in this phrase: "Your task assist in checking further advance by enemy in above areas [New Guinea–Solomons] by seizing favorable opportunities to destroy ships shipping and aircraft." The order is noteworthy in that Nimitz did not tell Fletcher how to accomplish the mission. This was totally up to Fletcher.

Nimitz issued detailed instructions to commanders on 29 April. By this time, additional intelligence was also provided to Fletcher. It now seemed all

The IJN operated a number of seaplane tenders that had no counterpart in the US Navy. Ten fast merchant ships were converted before the war to carry as many as 12 seaplanes, which could be launched with an onboard catapult and recovered by use of the ship's cranes. These ships were used to provide air cover for amphibious operations. *Kamikawa Maru* was assigned to the Covering Group. (*Ships of the World* Magazine)

but certain that the enemy intended to strike at both Port Moresby and Tulagi. Four primary groups had been identified to conduct this operation – an invasion force for both objectives, a support force, and the carrier force. At this point, the estimate of enemy carriers was refined to three.

To take on the Japanese, Fletcher had the carrier *Yorktown* that with her escorts of three cruisers and four destroyers comprised Task Force (TF)-17. After a short stop in Pearl Harbor beginning on March 26, the carrier *Lexington* (with her escorting two cruisers and five destroyers making up TF-11) was ordered to return to the South Pacific and rendezvous with Fletcher in the eastern Coral Sea on May 1. Fletcher would assume command of the combined carrier force. With his two carriers, Fletcher had the basic mission of covering Port Moresby and the Solomons. Since arriving in the South Pacific in February, Fletcher had considered striking the main Japanese base at Rabaul in an attempt to forestall any continued Japanese advance. He had dismissed this as too aggressive and not worth the risk. Even with two carriers, Fletcher continued his strategy of staying beyond the range of air searches from Rabaul (about 700 miles) and seeking favorable opportunities

A fine view of USS *New Orleans*, the lead ship in a class of seven heavy cruisers built between 1933 and 1936. These were the best of the US Navy's so-called Treaty cruisers and possessed the speed and endurance to act as carrier escorts. (US Naval Historical Center)

The 4,000-ton minelayer *Tsugaru*, completed in October 1941, was the flagship of Rear Admiral Abe's transport component of the MO Invasion Force. *Tsugaru* survived the Coral Sea and was later sunk by submarine attack in June 1944 after an active career. (Yamato Museum)

The *Kamikaze*-class destroyer *Asanagi* was assigned to the escort of the MO Invasion Force. Completed in 1924, her dated design is representative of the types of ships assigned to Inoue's 4th Fleet. (Yamato Museum)

to intercept Japanese forces moving into the Coral Sea or down the Solomons. After meeting with TF-11 on May 1 300 miles northwest of New Caledonia, Fletcher decided to move to a point 325 miles south of Guadalcanal to be prepared to react to any Japanese movement.

Supporting Fletcher was General Douglas MacArthur's Southwest Pacific Area Naval Forces organized into TF-44. These included the US heavy cruiser *Chicago* and one destroyer, the *Perkins*, from Noumea and the Australian cruisers *Australia* and *Hobart*, which had been refitting at Sydney. This force would rendezvous on May 4, 350 miles southwest of Guadalcanal, and come under Fletcher's overall control. Four US Navy submarines were also provided by MacArthur and assigned patrols in Japanese areas.

Though the Coral Sea is known as a carrier action, Fletcher (whose background was in cruisers) made preparation for surface gunnery action against the Japanese if the situation presented itself. He created two surface task groups that could be detached from the main force to operate independently. The first was based on the escorts of the two carrier groups and included five heavy cruisers and five destroyers. The second was centered on TF-44 and included two heavy cruisers (one Australian), the Australian light cruiser and two destroyers.

A vital part of the Allied defense was tasked to the Allied Air Force, Southwest Pacific Area. This force would provide Fletcher with long-range reconnaissance and the means to strike Japanese naval forces. On paper, it was a large force that looked ready to make a significant contribution. However, it was also a new force still dealing with command and control and readiness problems. On average, only 12–15 B-17s, nine–14 B-25s, 16 B-26s, ten RAAF Hudsons and three RAAF PBY Catalina flying boats were ready for operations. This would be adequate for searching the approaches to Port Moresby, but coverage of the upper Solomons and the eastern Coral Sea depended on retention of the seaplane base at Tulagi. In reality, these assets were of limited value to Fletcher as he did not control them, and was not even regularly informed of their activities.

One asset of potentially more value to Fletcher was a squadron of US Navy Catalina flying boats that arrived at Noumea on April 25. First in place was seaplane tender *Tangier* with six PBYs; six more arrived about May 3. However, based at Noumea, they were able to cover up only to the extreme southern part of the Solomons. The entire Allied order of battle for the battle of the Coral Sea can be found on pages 34–35.

Overall, Fletcher's plan was simple and showed flexibility. With half of the Pacific Fleet's operational carriers entrusted to him, he displayed a prudent combination of caution mixed with opportunistic aggressiveness. His focus was on protecting Port Moresby as it was here where the greatest threat seemed to be. He was hamstrung by inadequate air reconnaissance and logistical resources, but both were beyond his control. If there was a fault with his planning, it was the focus on the Coral Sea and the approaches to Port Moresby. No air searches were focused on the area east of the Solomons where, unknown to Fletcher, the greatest danger lay. Fletcher's deployment of his oilers was also faulty, again owing to his ignorance of a danger on his eastern flank.

What is often not realized about the American planning for Coral Sea was the extreme aggressiveness of Nimitz and King. Both Nimitz and King were overconfident regarding the capability of US carriers, and thus were willing to accept battle on inferior terms. While King was known for his aggression, Nimitz's role in the battle is often overlooked. Even when it appeared that the Japanese force would contain as many as four carriers, Nimitz was determined to bring the Japanese carrier forces in the Coral Sea to battle. If he could reduce their strength, the offensive power of the entire IJN would be blunted. Nimitz even decided to double his bet by sending TF-16 to the South Pacific after its return from the Tokyo raid, but this force could not arrive in the area until between May 14 and 16, likely when the battle was over. However, Nimitz's decision to put the entire striking power of the Pacific Fleet into the South Pacific was bold as it left Pearl Harbor uncovered by carriers. Had the battle of the Coral Sea continued, this decision would have paid handsome dividends as the arrival of the two fresh carriers would have surprised the Japanese who would have had nothing to counter them with.

The light cruiser *Tenryu* was assigned to the Covering Force. With her sister ship, *Tatsuta*, these were the oldest cruisers in service in the IJN in 1942, another indicator of the low priority given to the 4th Fleet. (Yamato Museum)

# THE BATTLE OF THE CORAL SEA

## OPENING MOVES

By the end of April, events in the South Pacific began to gain momentum. On April 28, the Japanese improvised a seaplane base at Shortland Island in the Solomons and moved five long-range H6K4 Type 97 flying boats (codenamed "Mavis" by the Allies) to the facility. These aircraft possessed a remarkable normal range of almost 3,000 miles and provided the Japanese commanders scouting coverage well into the Coral Sea. The next day, the Tulagi Invasion Force departed Rabaul and the Main Body (including *Shoho*) departed Truk. On May 1, the MO Carrier Striking Force left Truk.

The first blow of the battle was delivered on the morning of May 3 when the 3rd Kure Special Naval Landing Force landed unopposed on the islands of Tulagi and Gavutu. This move was supported by aircraft from Rabaul and the carrier *Shoho*, which had moved to a position 180 miles west of Tulagi to cover the landings.

Thus far, everything seemed to be running according to plan for the Japanese. However, by the end of May 3, the tightly synchronized MO plan was already running into trouble. The Carrier Striking Force was tasked with the seemingly simple mission of ferrying nine Zero fighters from Truk to Rabaul. This was to occur on May 2 when the carriers would be closest to Rabaul on their way south. However, when the nine fighters took off on schedule for Vunakanau Airfield on New Britain, they were forced to return to the carriers because of bad weather. An attempt to repeat the operation the following day was also thwarted by weather with one of the planes being lost in the attempt. The carriers were now two days behind schedule, yet the

The destroyer *Yugure* was one of four *Hatsuharu*-class destroyers in Destroyer Division 27 assigned to the MO Carrier Striking Force. Completed in 1935, *Yugure* carried six 24in. torpedo tubes and five 5in. guns, but only two triple 25mm mounts for protection against air attack. (Yamato Museum)

The *New Orleans*-class heavy cruiser *Astoria* was part of TF-17's screen during the battle of the Coral Sea. She served in the same capacity at Midway before being sunk by Japanese heavy cruisers at the battle of Savo Island in August 1942. (US Naval Historical Center)

Japanese never considered delaying the remainder of the operation. The Japanese viewed the delivery of the fighters with such importance because of the requirement to reinforce Rabaul's air strength, which was key to gaining air superiority over Port Moresby. This episode shows how little allowance was made in Japanese planning for even the smallest things to go wrong, as well as the basic weakness of a plan that hinged on a factor as small as nine fighters in the first place.

As the Japanese carriers attempted to complete their ferry mission, Fletcher was just getting reports of the occupation of Tulagi around 1900hrs on the evening of May 3. His forces were already at sea, waiting for word of any Japanese advance. Despite the fact that MacArthur's air force had provided no advance warning of the Tulagi invasion, here was information Fletcher could act on. Early on May 3, TF-17 was slowly moving westward into the central Coral Sea. Fletcher and TF-17 had become separated from *Lexington* as TF-11 completed its refueling. Actually, *Lexington* had completed refueling early and was close to Fletcher's position. Strict radio silence denied Fletcher this knowledge, so when reports came in of the invasion of Tulagi, he decided to react immediately with TF-17 alone. Fletcher turned his force north by 2030hrs and worked up to 27 knots to be in a position to attack Japanese forces off Tulagi at dawn on May 4. He was aware that this would reveal the presence of a US carrier in the area, but Fletcher was more concerned with surprising the Japanese and delivering some punishing blows.

# THE AMERICAN CARRIER RAID ON MAY 4

By May 4, the Tulagi Invasion Force was without air cover. *Shoho* had departed to move north to cover the Port Moresby invasion convoy then departing Rabaul and the MO Carrier Striking Force was still in the area of Rabaul attempting to complete its frustratingly difficult ferry mission. When American carrier aircraft appeared over the skies of Tulagi on the morning of May 4, the Japanese were caught completely by surprise and were essentially defenseless.

Northampton-class heavy cruiser Chester in August 1942. Chester was active early in the war as a carrier escort, including at the battle of the Coral Sea. Her port side 5in. gun battery can be seen pointed skyward. Armed with a total of eight 5in. guns, four 1.1in. quadruple automatic cannon mounts and a variable number of 20mm guns, the Northampton-class cruisers possessed an impressive anti-aircraft fit by early 1942 standards. (US Naval Historical Center)

At 0630hrs, *Yorktown* began launching what would be the first of four strikes. The first wave included 28 dive-bombers and 12 torpedo bombers. No fighter escort was provided as no air opposition was expected. The attack began at 0820hrs. Large targets were few with the large minelayer *Okinoshima* and two destroyers being the most valuable. The most notable result of the first strike was the damaging of destroyer *Kikuzuki*, which was later beached and lost. The same aircraft were turned around for a second strike with 27 dive-bombers and 11 torpedo bombers attacking again just after noon. Later, a third wave was sent in with 21 dive-bombers, departing *Yorktown* at 1400hrs and returning at 1630hrs. The results of this intense effort, and of a wave of four fighters launched to strafe the Type 97 flying boats located in Tulagi harbor, was very disappointing. Fletcher claimed that two destroyers, one freighter and four patrol craft had been sunk and a light cruiser driven aground. The real tally was much less. In addition to the destroyer *Kikuzuki*, three small minesweepers and four landing barges had been sunk. Perhaps the most important result was the destruction of the five Type 97 flying boats. Total Japanese casualties were 87 killed and 124 wounded.

The *Mutsuki*-class destroyer *Kikuzuki*, shown here beached in December 1944, was the largest Japanese ship sunk in *Yorktown*'s May 4 raid on Tulagi. Casualties among the ship's crew included 12 killed and 22 wounded. (US Naval Historical Center)

# MOVEMENT TO CONTACT: MAY 5–6

Following his strike against Tulagi, Fletcher headed south at high speed. The Japanese had no idea where the carrier was that mounted the raid, so Fletcher was easily able to escape retaliation. On the morning of May 5, he rendezvoused with TF-11 approximately 325 miles south of Guadalcanal. He now took his combined force to the southeast using the opportunity to refuel TF-17. Around 1100hrs, a Wildcat from *Yorktown* destroyed a Type 97 flying boat from Shortland. The Japanese aircraft did not have time to send a signal, but its destruction gave them a vague notion of the location of an American carrier.

Meanwhile, the Japanese carrier force was groping in the dark. The American raid on Tulagi found the Japanese carriers fueling north of the Solomons. In response to reports of the American attack, Takagi rushed his force to the southeast expecting to find an American carrier east of Tulagi. After finding nothing, Takagi confirmed his intention of entering the Coral Sea from an area east of the Solomons. On the evening of May 5, Takagi turned to the west after rounding San Cristobal Island in the southern Solomons. He planned to fuel on May 6 some 180 miles west of Tulagi before turning south into the Coral Sea. Thus throughout the day on May 5, neither carrier force had any real idea where the other was.

Fletcher was receiving extensive reporting from MacArthur's air units on the location and movement of a number of Japanese units active in the Solomon Sea. This included reports of carriers. On May 4 at around noon, an American bomber reported a force, with a carrier, off Bougainville. This was

*Kikuzuki* was one of two *Mutsuki*-class destroyers assigned to the Tulagi Invasion Force. The *Mutsuki* class was the first class of Japanese destroyer to carry the deadly 24in. torpedoes. As was the case with most early war Japanese destroyers, she carried a negligible anti-aircraft armament. (Yamato Museum)

# Movement of US and Japanese naval forces, May 2–6

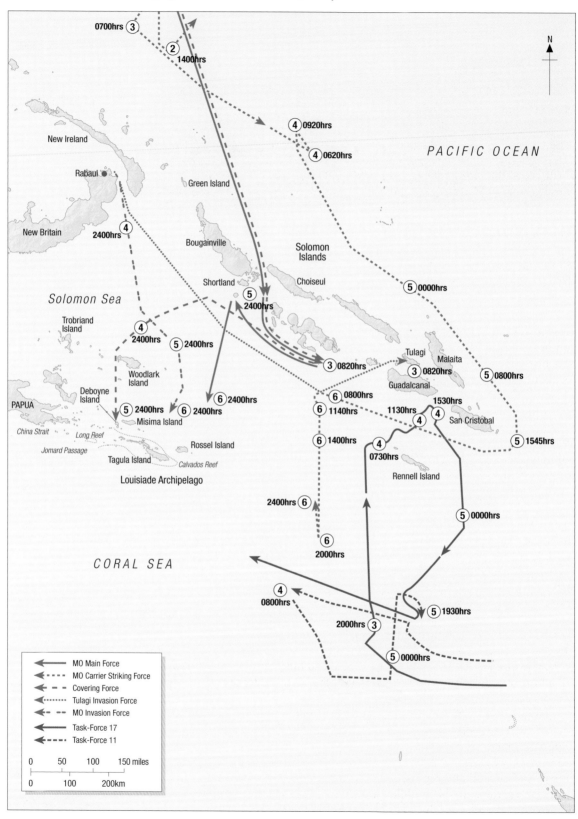

N

0700hrs ③

② 1400hrs

④ 0920hrs

④ 0620hrs

PACIFIC OCEAN

New Ireland

Rabaul ●

Green Island

New Britain

④ 2400hrs

Bougainville

Solomon Islands

Shortland

Choiseul

⑤ 0000hrs

⑤ 2400hrs

Solomon Sea

Trobriand Island

④ 2400hrs

⑤ 2400hrs

Woodlark Island

Deboyne Island

PAPUA

⑤ 2400hrs

⑥ 2400hrs

Misima Island

China Strait

Long Reef

Jomard Passage

Rossel Island

Tagula Island

Calvados Reef

Louisiade Archipelago

Tulagi

Malaita

③ 0820hrs

③ 0820hrs

⑤ 0800hrs

Guadalcanal

1530hrs

⑥ 0800hrs

⑥ 1140hrs

1130hrs

④

④

San Cristobal

⑥ 1400hrs

④ 0730hrs

⑤ 1545hrs

Rennell Island

⑥ 2400hrs

④ 2400hrs

③ 0820hrs

2400hrs ⑥

⑥ 2000hrs

⑤ 0000hrs

CORAL SEA

④ 0800hrs

⑤ 1930hrs

2000hrs ③

⑤ 0000hrs

MO Main Force
MO Carrier Striking Force
Covering Force
Tulagi Invasion Force
MO Invasion Force
Task-Force 17
Task-Force 11

0    50    100    150 miles
0    100    200km

50

The light carrier *Shoho* was attacked on the morning of May 7 by a total of 93 aircraft from two American carriers. Within 15 minutes, the carrier was ripped apart by some 13 bombs and at least seven torpedo hits. *Shoho* quickly sank with heavy loss of life. (US Naval Historical Center)

eventually reported to Fletcher as a *Kaga*-class carrier. On May 5, another report was issued of a Japanese carrier operating southwest of Bougainville. What MacArthur's airmen had sighted was the *Shoho* headed north to cover the MO Invasion Force, which had departed Rabaul on May 4.

On May 6, Fletcher exercised his authority from Nimitz to merge all three task forces into TF-17. His total strength was two carriers, eight cruisers (two Australian) and 11 destroyers. Fletcher ordered his combined force to head southeast throughout the day to refuel in deteriorating weather. No contact was made by TF-17's scouting dive-bombers, though one Dauntless ended its planned track a mere 20 miles from the Japanese carriers operating south of New Georgia. Just after noon, MacArthur's airmen reported a carrier and four other warships southwest of Bougainville. Fletcher's afternoon scout missions flying 275 miles north and northwest of TF-17 located nothing. With the Allied Air Forces' reconnaissance efforts still focused on the Solomon Sea and the Louisiades, Fletcher remained ignorant of the true location of the Japanese carrier force, now located to his northeast.

At 1015hrs on May 6, radar revealed the presence of a snooper in the area of TF-17 that fighters on CAP were unable to locate. Fletcher now had to assume that his position was compromised. With no intelligence generated by his own scouts, Fletcher had to assume that the numerous contact reports from Allied Air Forces aircraft confirmed the signals intelligence he had been receiving from Nimitz which indicated that Japanese carriers were tasked to strike Port Moresby on May 7 and that the Japanese invasion convoy would transit the Louisiades at the Jomard Passage on May 7 or 8. However, the Americans had yet actually to sight the invasion convoy, and of course, Fletcher remained ignorant of the actual location of the Japanese carriers. On the evening of May 6, Fletcher brought TF-17 to the northwest and increased speed to 21 knots. He aimed to be 170 miles southeast of Deboyne Island on the morning of May 7 to strike the Japanese forces reported off Misima Island in the central Louisiades.

The Japanese were the first to get solid information on the location of the enemy carriers. At 1030hrs, the aircraft spotted by TF-17 radar (actually a Type 97 flying boat) reported TF-17 420 miles southwest of Tulagi. However, the aircraft provided an incorrect position (off by 50 miles) and an incorrect course and speed. The report, received by Takagi at 1050hrs, caught the Japanese carriers in the middle of fueling. The American carriers were reportedly 350 miles south (actually 300 miles). Not until 1200hrs were the two carriers, escorted by two destroyers, released to head south to chase the contact. Hara decided not to launch a long-range strike or mount his own air search not wanting to reveal his presence to the Americans. He continued to head south until 1930hrs on May 6, coming to within 60–70 miles of TF-17.

May 6 was a day of missed opportunities for both sides. While US carrier planes had just missed spotting their main opponents in the morning, Hara continued to play a passive game of ambush and failed to follow up aggressively on the solid lead given him by Japanese long-range search planes. Even after this lead went cold at least Hara had a general idea of the location of the American carriers. On the other hand, Fletcher continued to believe that the Japanese carriers were operating to his northwest. With both forces continuing to close, a clash on May 7 was all but certain, and there was a grave potential that the Japanese carriers could unleash a deadly ambush on their unsuspecting opponents.

## THE CLASHES OF MAY 7

On the morning of May 7, TF-17 was positioned approximately 150 miles south of Rossel Island. This placed it between the two main Japanese forces. The MO Invasion Force was located north of the Jomard Passage with Goto's Main Force located northwest of the convoy. The MO Carrier Striking Force was operating approximately 300 miles southwest of Tulagi, which placed it approximately 200 miles southeast of Fletcher. Fletcher was focused on striking the Japanese force operating in the Solomon Sea including the Japanese carriers he assumed were located somewhere south of Bougainville. He still had no idea of the true location of the main Japanese carrier force. The Japanese also found themselves in a not entirely favorable position. While they still hoped to stage an ambush on the unsuspecting American carriers, they had yet to adjust the MO plan to the fact that the Carrier Striking Force was behind schedule and that an American carrier force was

A Douglas Devastator from USS *Enterprise* over Wake Island on February 24, 1942. The highlight of the Devastator's early war career was at the Coral Sea when the aircraft put several torpedoes into the Japanese light carrier *Shoho*. A month later at the battle of Midway, the aircraft's true vulnerability was revealed. (US Naval Historical Center)

now blocking the advance of the Invasion Force and was closer to the transport force than were the Japanese carriers. Inoue had yet to adjust the movement of the invasion convoy and its continued advance southward now made it vulnerable to American air strikes. While Fletcher had the option of waiting and reacting to Japanese moves, the Japanese would have to force a decision quickly if the operation was to stay on schedule.

For both sides, the key to success was reconnaissance. On May 7, both commanders were severely let down by the efforts of their reconnaissance aircraft and crews and these series of mistakes would shape the battle. Allied Air Forces' aircraft continued to focus their efforts on the area north of the Louisiades and into the Solomon Sea. Fletcher augmented this with the dispatch of 10 Dauntlesses from *Yorktown* at 0600hrs. These were assigned sectors from the northwest through the east out to 250 miles. The Japanese also made a large-scale scouting effort. Aircraft from Rabaul, the Shortlands, Tulagi and the newly created seaplane base on Deboyne Island would search south of the Louisiades. Meanwhile, no longer trusting in the efficiency of land-based searches alone, Hara decided to use 12 B5N carrier attack aircraft to search from 160 to 270 degrees out to a distance of 250 miles from his force. The first side to receive solid contact reports would probably be the first to launch its strike, thus grabbing victory.

Also at dawn on May 7, Fletcher decided to detach TG-17.3 under the command of British Rear Admiral J. G. Crace. Under his command Crace had his three cruisers, and with the addition of another American destroyer, a total of three destroyers. Crace's mission was to prevent the MO Invasion Force from passing south of the Louisiades. This was a controversial move as it removed one third of Fletcher's already weak carrier screen and placed a force with no air cover within range of Japanese land-based aircraft. It was also debatable that the force could accomplish its mission at all. If the carrier battle went badly for the Americans, the Japanese would have little difficulty sweeping aside Crace's force. On the other hand, if the carrier battle went well for the Americans, the Japanese would have to suspend the invasion anyway. Fletcher's rationale was that if the carrier battle neutralized both forces, as often happened in US Navy prewar exercises, then Crace would be positioned to contest the Japanese advance into the Coral Sea. Under the circumstances, this seemed a good insurance move by Fletcher, especially given that the anti-aircraft contribution by Crace's ships to the defense of TF-17's carriers was minimal.

A fine view of the heavy cruiser *Furutaka* in 1939 following modernization. *Furutaka* and her sister ship *Kako* both survived the Coral Sea but were both lost during the fierce battles around Guadalcanal later in 1942. (Yamato Museum)

# Movement of US and Japanese naval forces, May 7

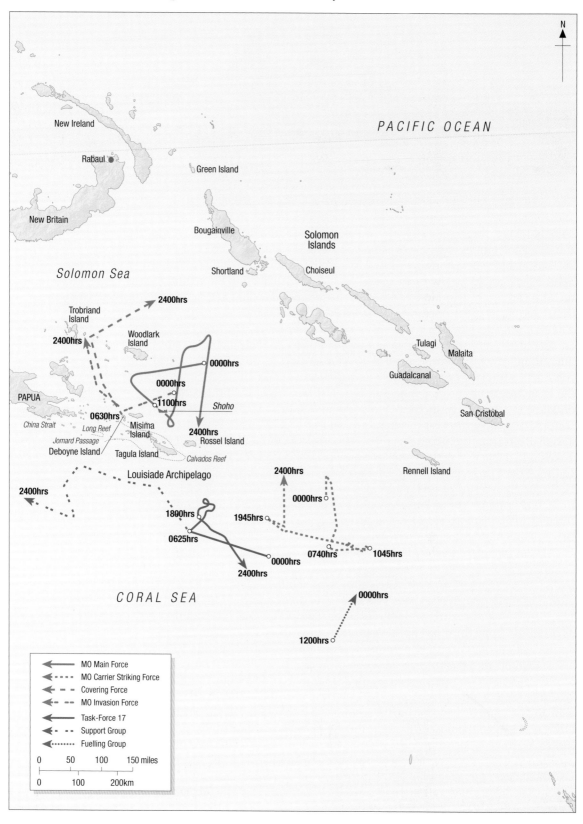

N

PACIFIC OCEAN

New Ireland

Rabaul

Green Island

New Britain

Bougainville

Solomon Islands

Solomon Sea

Shortland

Choiseul

2400hrs

Trobriand Island

Woodlark Island

2400hrs

Tulagi

Malaita

Guadalcanal

0000hrs

0000hrs

1100hrs

Shoho

PAPUA

China Strait

0630hrs

Long Reef

Misima Island

Jomard Passage

Deboyne Island

Tagula Island

Calvados Reef

2400hrs

Rossel Island

San Cristobal

Louisiade Archipelago

2400hrs

2400hrs

0000hrs

Rennell Island

1800hrs

1945hrs

0625hrs

0740hrs

1045hrs

0000hrs

2400hrs

CORAL SEA

0000hrs

1200hrs

| | |
|---|---|
| ← | MO Main Force |
| ←---- | MO Carrier Striking Force |
| ← - - | Covering Force |
| ← -- -- | MO Invasion Force |
| ← | Task-Force 17 |
| ← - · - · | Support Group |
| ← ······ | Fuelling Group |

0        50       100      150 miles

0        100      200km

Given the relatively small area of operations and the numbers of ships and aircraft in motion, contact reports quickly filtered up to the respective commanders. Hara was the first to receive a solid contact report and his subsequent actions will be dealt with first. His 12 scout aircraft had departed at 0600hrs and were focused on the area south and southwest of his position. What Hara did not know was that Fletcher was closer to his force than he thought (just over 200 miles), and that he had moved north and the Japanese carrier-borne search effort was off the mark. This mattered little to Hara when at 0722hrs, two Type 97 carrier attack planes from *Shokaku* reported an American force of one carrier, one cruiser and three destroyers only 163 miles south of the Japanese carriers. Later, an oiler and a cruiser was reported some 25 miles southeast of the carrier. This was the information that the Japanese had been waiting days for and it fitted perfectly with Hara's estimate of where the Americans should be. Hara sent another carrier attack plane to confirm the report and made preparations to launch a full strike. By 0815hrs, a total of 78 aircraft (18 fighters, 24 torpedo bombers and 26 dive-bombers) were on their way to destroy the carrier under the command of Lieutenant-Commander Takahashi Kakuichi.

What appeared to be a promising situation for the Japanese quickly turned into a potential disaster. Upon arriving at the reported contact just after 0900hrs, Takahashi found only the oiler and its escort. An enlarged search of the area found nothing. Things got worse when Hara received reports from a floatplane from the cruiser *Kinugasa* (part of the MO Main Force)

The Royal Australian Navy (RAN) heavy cruiser *Australia* was the flagship of Rear Admiral Crace during the battle. *Australia* was a *County*-class Treaty cruiser completed in 1928 for the RAN by the British. Her main armament consisted of eight 8in guns. This view was taken in August 1942. (US Naval Historical Center)

The Mitsubishi A5M Type 96 carrier fighter was the IJN's standard shipborne fighter until the advent of the A6M Type 0 fighter. Four of these obsolescent aircraft were assigned to the *Shoho* Air Group for the MO Operation. (*Ships of the World* Magazine)

USS *Sims* in May 1940. Completed in 1938, she was the lead ship of her class, which was often used for carrier-screening duties early in the war. Main armament was five 5in. guns and 12 21in. torpedo tubes. During the battle, she was caught alone and quickly overwhelmed by Japanese dive-bombers. (US Naval Historical Center)

searching south of the Louisiades that it had spotted American carriers southeast of Rossel Island. The force consisted of a *Saratoga*-class carrier and a second carrier, and at 1008hrs they were in the process of launching a strike. At 1051hrs, the original searchers from *Shokaku* returned and revealed that they had only seen an oiler. Faced with this alarming turn of events, Hara recalled his strike at 1100hrs.

Before leaving the area Takahashi unleashed his dive-bombers on the only targets in view. The first four Type 99 carrier bombers selected the destroyer *Sims* as their target and quickly destroyed her with three hits by 550-pound bombs. The destroyer sank by the stern suffering heavy loss of life. The oiler *Neosho* was the target of over 30 dive-bombers, which straddled her 15 times and gained seven hits. One carrier bomber was shot down during the 18-minute attack. The ship was left listing, aflame and without power.

USS *Neosho* refueling *Yorktown* on May 1. *Neosho* was bombed by Japanese carrier aircraft on May 7 and was finally scuttled on May 11. Throughout the battle, Fletcher devoted considerable attention to maintaining proper fuel levels for his forces. (US Naval Historical Center)

However, half the crew re-boarded the ship and put out the fires and was later saved by an American destroyer after the battle. The tanker was finally scuttled and the remaining crew rescued on May 11.

The Japanese had squandered an opportunity to ambush the Americans and had sunk only two minor ships in return. The last of the strike had not returned until after 1500hrs, so the prospects of launching another strike that day on the real American carriers looked doubtful. Fortunately for Hara, the strike on the oiler group did not fatally compromise his position. Later in the day, Fletcher was aware that *Neosho* had been attacked, but neither ship had radioed a distress signal before it was sunk or put out of action. *Sims* had sent an aircraft contact report, but it was not picked up by TF-17. The only word from *Neosho* was at 1021hrs that she was under attack by three aircraft. Since this could have been from long-range aircraft from Tulagi, Fletcher and his staff were still unaware that a large carrier-based strike had destroyed his supporting oiler.

As the Japanese struggled to clarify their situation, an almost identical situation developed for the Americans. However, in their case, circumstances developed more favorably. As early as 0735hrs, Fletcher received word from his scouts of Japanese activity. The first sighting was of two cruisers northwest of Rossel Island. This report was followed by a contact at 0815hrs of two carriers and four cruisers north of Misima Island. The location of the force was 225 miles northwest of TF-17, which put it beyond the range of the fighters and torpedo planes. However, with the Japanese force reported moving south and Fletcher moving north, a full attack was judged to be possible. Fletcher waited over an hour to launch, but beginning at 0926hrs, *Lexington* began to put her strike of ten fighters, 28 dive-bombers and 12 torpedo bombers into the air. At 0944hrs, *Yorktown* began the first of two launches, committing eight fighters, 25 dive-bombers and ten torpedo bombers to the attack.

However, as soon as the planes were headed north, things began to go wrong. Throughout the morning, radar had reported air contacts in the vicinity of the task force. Though fighters were unable to locate the snoopers, Fletcher assumed, correctly, that he had been located. Added to this, was the report from *Neosho* at 1021hrs that she was under attack. Worse still, the return of the scout plane that had reported the two carriers revealed that the actual report had meant to report the spotting of four light cruisers and two

The light cruiser *Yubari* was present at the Coral Sea as flagship of Destroyer Flotilla 6. This ship was completed in 1923 as an experimental design to mount the armament of a 5,000-ton light cruiser on a hull of only 2,900 tons. (Yamato Museum)

**AMERICAN FORCES:**

*Lexington* Air Group
1. *Lexington* Air Group command section (three SBD) and two VF-2 F4F fighters
2. VS-2 (ten SBD-3)
3. VB-2 (15 SBD-2/3) and four VF-2 F4F fighters
4. VT-2 (12 TBD-1) and four VF-2 F4F fighters
   *Yorktown* Air Group
5. VS-5 (17 SBD-3) and three VF-42 fighters
6. VB-5 (eight SBD-3)
7. VT-5 (ten TBD-1) and five VF-42 F4F fighters

▼ EVENTS

**Attack of the Lexington Air Group**

**1.** 1040hrs: *Shoho* spotted 40 miles to the north. Commander Ault prepares a coordinated attack. His command element and VS-2 head straight into an attack on the carrier to soften its defenses. VB-2 swings to the east to mount a coordinated attack with the slower Devastators of VT-2.

**2.** 1110hrs: Ault begins dive from 10,000ft. All three command section aircraft miss.

**3.** 1110–1117hrs: VS-2 moves around to north to take advantage of sun and wind direction and then dives from 12,500 feet against light antiaircraft fire. Two Japanese A5M fighters attack the lead elements with no result. *Shoho* continues a turn to port to complete a circle making VS-2 attack from astern. Ten aircraft drop 500-pound bombs at 2,000ft but all miss. The single A6M fighter on CAP damages one SBD on its dive and shoots down another while pulling out of its dive. The two A5Ms attack and damage several SBDs after completion of the attack. A single VS-2 aircraft attempts a second dive on an escort ship with its 110-pound bombs without success.

**4.** 1118hrs: VB-3 starts dive from 12,000ft, just as *Shoho* completes her second full circle. Attacked by an A5M on the way down, the squadron commander, LCDR Hamilton, scores a 1,000-pound bomb hit just forward of the elevator. One additional hit is scored further forward. Massive fires break out on *Shoho*'s hangar deck fed by fueled aircraft. No Dauntlesses are lost.

**5.** 1115–1119hrs: VT-2 descends from 4,000ft to 100ft to release torpedoes. *Shoho* sights aircraft off starboard quarter and turns to starboard to avoid. VT-2 heads through gap between two cruisers to attack the carrier on her beam. When *Shoho* continues a port turn, the squadron is set up for an anvil attack. Two A5M fighters attack torpedo planes on final approach, but are intercepted by Wildcats.

**6.** 1119hrs: VT-2 commanding officer launches first torpedo from *Shoho*'s port quarter. Five hits are scored (nine are claimed) and includes a hit which disables *Shoho*'s steering keeping the ship on a southeasterly course. The torpedo damage is fatal, creating a list and uncontrolled flooding.

**Attack of the *Yorktown* Air Group**

**7.** 1125hrs: the commander of the dive-bombers decides to press his attack immediately without waiting for the slower torpedo planes. Seventeen VS-5 aircraft attack with 1,000-pound bombs claiming nine hits against the non-maneuvering *Shoho*. Three A6Ms attack with no effect.

**8.** 1130hrs: eight VB-5 SBDs attack, claiming six hits. The Japanese confirm that as many as 11 hits were scored by *Yorktown* dive-bombers. The last *Yorktown* aircraft actually attacks a cruiser when it is evident that *Shoho* is doomed. Two VB-5 aircraft are damaged by A6Ms.

**9.** 1129hrs: VT-5 begins attack on *Shoho*'s starboard side. All ten aircraft claim hits; the Japanese confirm two but more are likely. Two A5M fighters attack the vulnerable Devastators after their attack. Both are shot down by escorting Wildcats and another Zero is also destroyed.

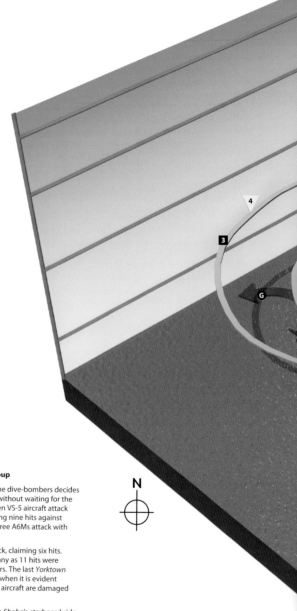

# THE US CARRIER AIRCRAFT ATTACK ON JAPANESE CARRIER SHO

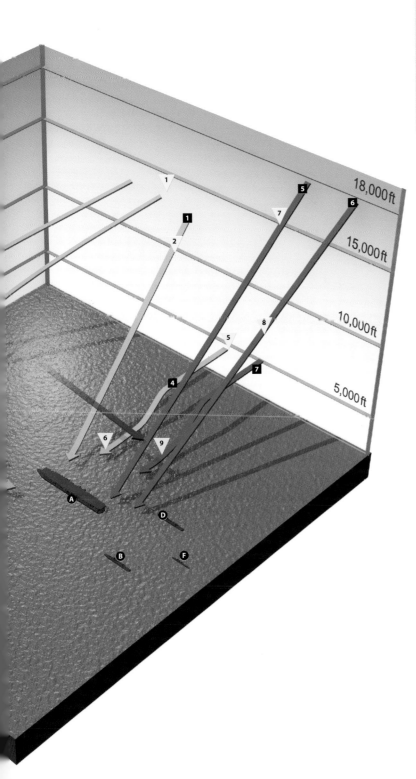

**JAPANESE FORCES:**
**A** *Shoho*
**B** *Furutaka*
**C** *Kinugasa*
**D** *Kako*
**E** *Aoba*
**F** Destroyer *Sazanami*
**G** CAP on station before attack began
(one A6M Zero and A5M Type 96 Claude)
**H** CAP launched at 1107hrs (three A6M Zero)

18,000 ft

15,000 ft

10,000 ft

5,000 ft

7 MAY

destroyers. Confronted with the same dilemma that Hara had faced, Fletcher declined to recall his strike. He knew from Allied Air Forces' reporting that there was heavy Japanese activity in the planned strike area. The situation brightened when Fletcher received a report at 1022hrs from Port Moresby that two hours earlier a B-17 had reported a large force including a carrier, ten transports and 16 other ships just south of the false carrier report. Fletcher passed this new information to the airborne strikes and let them proceed to the target area in the hope that they would find suitable targets.

While Fletcher was concerned he had missed the main Japanese carrier force, his strike was headed into an area rich with targets. With the MO Invasion Force and the Main Force all located fairly close together and the weather in the area very clear, there was no chance the Americans' strike would be entirely fruitless. In response to the American air activity, Inoue had turned the invasion convoy to the north to avoid air attack. He knew his force had been spotted and that American carriers were located to the southeast. He also had received reports of a force of two battleships a cruiser and four destroyers (Crace's force) located south of the Jomard Passage. Until Hara's carriers could deal with these threats, he stopped his advance. In the meantime, *Shoho* would have to defend his force from expected air attack.

# DEATH OF A CARRIER

Located in clear weather, and with a total of 93 American aircraft headed her way, *Shoho*'s first and last battle was destined to be a quick one. *Lexington*'s aircraft spotted her around 1040hrs about 40 miles to the north. *Shoho* had just landed her four-plane CAP and a carrier attack plane, and was preparing to launch a small strike on TF-17. When the American strike was spotted at 1050hrs, a total of one Type 0 and two Type 96 fighters were airborne.

*Lexington*'s air group was the first to attack and conducted one of the best-coordinated attacks by any US carrier during the entire war. The air group commander, Commander William Ault, opted to lead his command element and VS-2 straight in against the carrier to soften its defenses while the remainder of the air group set up for a coordinated attack. Opening the attack at 1110hrs, Ault's three dive-bombers all missed. *Shoho* conducted a sharp turn to port to evade her attackers, and this was successful in making all ten VS-2 aircraft miss as well. Japanese anti-aircraft fire was ineffective as were the attempts of the two Type 96 fighters against the diving Dauntlesses. The single Type 0 fighter on patrol was able to damage a Dauntless during its dive and shoot down a dive-bomber pulling out of its dive. At 1118hrs, VB-2 commenced its attack and scored two hits forward with 1,000-pound bombs. These caused massive fires on the hangar deck that were fed by the fueled aircraft being readied for the strike against TF-17. Simultaneously with the dive-bomber attack, VT-2 descended to its attack altitude of 100ft. Finding a gap in the cruiser screen, the commander of the squadron dropped his torpedo at 1119hrs. Five hits were gained, enough to cause fatal damage owing to uncontrolled flooding.

Lacking an overall strike commander, the *Yorktown*'s aircraft arrived to begin their attack on the listing and smoking *Shoho* though it should have been apparent she was already doomed. Beginning at 1125hrs, 24 of 25 dive-bombers from VB-5 and VS-5 attacked *Shoho*. Fifteen hits were claimed against the non-maneuvering target and Japanese sources confirm as many as

A remarkable action shot of *Shoho* under attack by American torpedo bombers on May 7. *Shoho* is already burning from dive-bombing damage. A Devastator can be seen turning away at right as its torpedo strikes the water below. (US Naval Historical Center)

11 hits. This brought *Shoho* dead in the water. At 1129hrs, VT-2 torpedo planes attacked and claimed ten hits. Japanese confirmed two, but more were likely. *Shoho* had been literally torn apart by a barrage of bombs and torpedoes. Of her crew of 834, only 203 survived. US losses were one Dauntless from *Yorktown* and two from *Lexington*.

By 1450hrs, both American air groups had recovered and were spotted on their carriers for additional strikes. Fletcher's aviators had done a good day's work, sinking the first Japanese carrier of the war. Given the impossibility of launching and recovering a strike before dark, and the bad weather in the area, Fletcher decided not to launch a second strike against Japanese units in the Solomon Sea or to launch additional searches for the main Japanese carrier force. Fletcher was aware of Inoue's retreat with the invasion convoy, but was still unaware of the location of the Japanese carriers. He was relieved that his misstep earlier in the day did not bring a punishing Japanese carrier strike.

While Fletcher may have escaped a Japanese air attack, TG-17.3 did not. Crace's force was operating throughout the day to the southeast of the Jomard Passage, placing it within range of Japanese land-based aircraft from Rabaul. Crace's force had been spotted earlier in the day, and at 1400hrs two

*Lexington*'s air group was the first to attack *Shoho*. Shown here is one of the five torpedo hits scored by *Lexington* Devastators. The ship is already burning as the result of two 1,000-pound hits. (US Naval Historical Center)

## THE AMERICAN CARRIER AIR ATTACK ON 7 MAY AGAINST *SHOHO* (pp. 62–63)

After dodging the bombs of the first 13 *Lexington* dive-bombers to attack, the *Shoho*'s luck began to run out. At 1118hrs, the commanding officer of VB-2, Lieutenant-Commander Weldon Hamilton (**1**), led his squadron into a dive from 12,000ft on the desperately maneuvering Japanese light carrier. The ship continued a hard turn to port and completed her second full circle. Though Hamilton was attacked by a Japanese Type 96 fighter during his dive, at 2,500ft he released his 1,000-pound bomb which impacted on the center of *Shoho*'s flight deck just forward of the aft elevator (**2**). This was the first American damage on *Shoho* and the first scored on any Japanese carrier in the entire war. Hamilton's squadron scored an additional bomb hit, which caused massive fires to break out on *Shoho*'s hangar deck fed by fueled aircraft being prepared for a strike. The ship was subjected to a further deluge of torpedoes and bombs from other *Lexington* and *Yorktown* aircraft and sank shortly thereafter with a heavy loss of life.

waves of G3M Type 96 attack bomber (Allied codename "Nell") aircraft arrived from Rabaul to deliver attacks. In the first wave, 12 G3Ms equipped with torpedoes were unsuccessful in scoring a single hit when they launched at excessive range. Five aircraft were lost. Approximately a half hour later, 19 additional G3Ms delivered a high-altitude bomb attack, again scoring no hits. Crace's skillful maneuvering and heavy anti-aircraft fire had avoided disaster, but the Japanese were still confident they had scored heavily. They claimed a *California*-class battleship and an *Augusta*-class cruiser sunk, a *Warspite*-class battleship heavily damaged and possible damage to a *Canberra*-class cruiser. Both the skill and the recognition abilities of the Japanese aviators were dismal and contrasted poorly with the Japanese Naval Air Force strikes of only a few months earlier, when land-based aircraft had quickly sunk the Royal Navy's capital ships *Prince of Wales* and *Repulse* off Malaya in the first few days of the war.

With the loss of *Shoho*, Inoue delayed the Port Moresby landings by two days. He moved the invasion convoy out of range and concentrated his surface combatants off Rossel Island to prepare for a possible night attack. Realizing this was not realistic, he later instructed Goto to split his cruiser force and keep two ships with the Main Force and send the other two to aid the Carrier Striking Force. The attack on *Shoho* did succeed in putting a greater sense of urgency into Takagi and Hara. Given the number of aircraft involved in the attack on *Shoho*, it was clear that two American carriers were on the loose. With the MO Operation in shambles, everything depended on the ability of the Carrier Striking Force to sweep the American carriers from the scene and get the operation back on schedule. Accordingly, Hara was now inclined to take risks. Since he had received no recent locating data on the American carriers, Hara ordered a search from the southwest to northwest out to 200 miles. These aircraft were launched at 1530hrs but gained no contact before being ordered to return. This search was intended to guide a risky dusk strike by the most experienced Japanese crews. From *Zuikaku*, nine carrier attack aircraft and six carrier bomber crews were selected to participate, joined by six more carrier attack aircraft and six carrier bombers from *Shokaku*. The fact that there was more than a small degree of desperation involved in this venture was obvious. Some of the crews had just returned from a seven-hour strike earlier in the day and now these crews were expected to take off again in increasingly terrible weather conditions to conduct a strike against an unlocated target.

*Haguro* was assigned to the MO Carrier Striking Force. With four dual 5in. mounts and four 25mm dual mounts, the *Myoko*-class cruisers were only marginally capable of providing anti-aircraft screening to the carriers. (Yamato Museum)

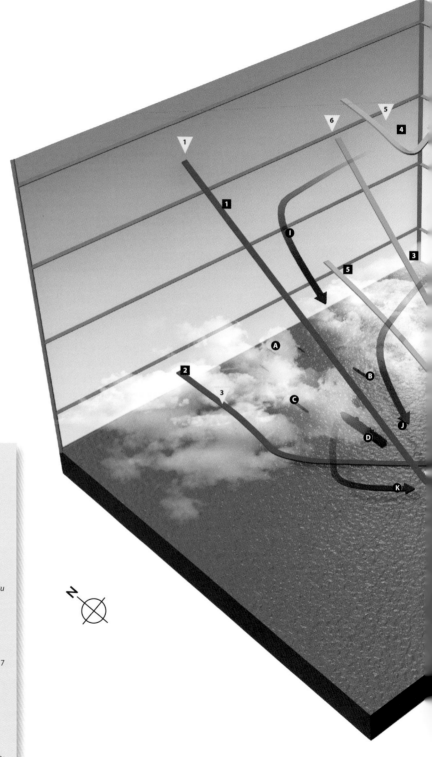

**JAPANESE FORCES:**
**A** Destroyers (three)
**B** *Myoko*
**C** *Haguro*
**D** *Zuikaku*
**E** *Shokaku*
**F** *Kinugasa*
**G** *Furutaka*
**H** A6M Zero CAP (three above *Shokaku*
at 13,000ft)
**I** A6M Zero CAP (three above *Zuikaku*
at 20,000ft)
**J** A6M Zero CAP (three launched from *Shokaku*
at 1049hrs)
**K** A6M Zero CAP (four launched from *Zuikaku*
at 1049hrs)

**AMERICAN FORCES:**
**1** *Yorktown* dive-bomber group (seven VS-5, 17
VB-5 SBDs and two VF-42 fighters)
**2** *Yorktown* torpedo plane group (nine VT-5
TBDs escorted by four VF-42 fighters)
**3** *Lexington* command section (four SBDs
(Commander Ault's aircraft plus three from
VS-2, escorted by two VF-2 fighters)
**4** *Lexington* dive-bomber group (11 VB-2 SBD
escorted by three VF-2 fighters)
**5** *Lexington* torpedo plane group (11 VT-2 TBDs
escorted by four VF-2 fighters)

20,000ft

15,000ft

10,000ft

5,000ft

H

F

G

## ▼ EVENTS

*Yorktown* **Air Group attack**

**1.** 1049hrs: *Yorktown* SBDs wait at 17,000ft southeast of Japanese carriers for VT-5 to arrive at attack position for coordinated attack. American aircraft are finally spotted by Japanese who launch seven ready CAP aircraft.

**2.** 1100hrs: Dive-bombers attack; only *Shokaku* is visible at this time. All seven VS-5 aircraft miss in large measure due to fogged sights and windscreens as they encounter warm, moist air at 8,000ft. Attacked by three *Zuikaku* A6Ms at 11,000ft; several SBDs are damaged, one badly. Four additional *Zuikaku* A6Ms, just launched, attack the SBDs as they withdraw.

1103hrs: VB-5 begins dive. Rear division attacked by A6Ms from *Shokaku* CAP and SBDs encounter same fogging problem.

1105hrs: First hit on the *Shokaku*'s port side forward creating fire on her bow. Second hit is scored on starboard side near island that ignites additional fires on flight and hangar decks. Hit is scored by Lt. John Powers who takes his SBD well under 1,000ft to ensure a hit.

**3.** 1103hrs: VT-5 starts attack on port beam and bow of *Shokaku* flying at 110 knots at 50ft. Attacks by six A6Ms (three each from *Shokaku* and *Zuikaku*) are defeated by VF-42 and at least one A6M is shot down.

**4.** 1108hrs: VT-5 releases torpedoes 1,000–2,000 yards from *Shokaku* just as VB-5 is finishing its attack. No hits are scored; one TBD damaged by anti-aircraft fire.

*Lexington* **Air Group attack**

**5.** 1130hrs: the *Lexington* strike spots the MO Carrier Striking Force after executing a box search after failing to find the enemy at the briefed position. The squadrons in *Lexington*'s strike became separated in the bad weather. Only four dive-bombers, 11 torpedo planes escorted by six fighters are available to attack. At this point, the Japanese have 11 A6Ms on CAP. *Shokaku* has four A6Ms at 13,000ft; *Zuikaku* has three fighters at 19,000ft and four more at low altitude assigned to watch for torpedo planes

**6.** 1140hrs: Ault's four SBDs attack first to draw Japanese CAP to protect the slow TBDs. The dive-bombers choose to conduct a glide-bomb attack as they are not at the proper altitude for a dive-bomb attack. The three high *Zuikaku* A6Ms attack the SBDs at 5,500ft, but three of the four dive-bombers drop their 1,000-pound bombs (one hangs on the aircraft) and one hit is scored. The two escorting Wildcats cover their retreat. In the fighter clash, one *Shokaku* A6M is shot down with one Wildcat possibly destroyed.

**7.** 1142–1150hrs: VT-2 attacks escorted by four Wildcats. The four *Zuikaku* A6Ms at low altitude shoot down two Wildcats, but are unable to get to the TBDs. The first two TBDs come in on *Shokaku*'s port bow. In response, *Shokaku* executes a hard turn to starboard to present her stern to the torpedo planes. Despite dropping from only 400–600 yards, both miss. The remainder of VT-2 attacks *Shokaku* from her starboard side after *Shokaku* completed a 180-degree turn. *Shokaku* turns away to outrun these torpedoes and all miss.

# THE US CARRIER AIRCRAFT ATTACK ON THE JAPANESE MO CARRIER STRIKING FORCE DIVISION ON 8 MAY

Predictably, the operation did not go well. The aircraft left the decks of their carriers starting at 1615hrs and were briefed to go to a point 280 miles west to search for the enemy. Unknown to the Japanese, the American carriers were only some 150 miles to the west-northwest but hidden under heavy clouds. When the Japanese strike arrived at its designated area, nothing was there. After an incomplete reconnaissance of the area, the aircraft headed home in three groups after jettisoning their ordnance. On their return, the Japanese ran afoul of the US carriers. Wildcats directed by radar intercepted the first group, and six carrier attack planes and one carrier bomber were shot down for the loss of three Wildcats. The second and third group arrived over the American carriers in the dark and, certain they were their own ships, attempted to land. Anti-aircraft fire from the Americans accounted for one carrier attack plane and cleared up any confusion on the part of the Japanese. Finally, by 2300hrs, the Japanese aircraft recovered with one additional carrier attack plane ditching. Of the 27 aircraft launched, 18 returned, a remarkable achievement. However, the loss of eight precious carrier attack planes would be felt the next day. Once debriefed, the Japanese aviators reported that TF-17 was a mere 40–60 miles to the west. Both sides now knew the other was close. The next day would certainly bring the deciding clash of the battle.

## PRE-BATTLE PREPARATIONS: MAY 8

Both sides knew that quick and accurate reconnaissance was the key to deciding events on May 8. During the night, both sides attempted to place themselves in a favorable position for the forthcoming battle. The American carriers moved southeast until after midnight and then turned to the west. The destroyer *Monaghan* was detached to rescue survivors from *Neosho* and *Sims*. This left TF-17 with seven destroyers. Crace ordered his force to head west in order to remain southeast of Port Moresby in position to intercept any Japanese forces advancing on Port Moresby in the wake of the carrier battle.

On the morning of May 8, TF-17 possessed 117 operational aircraft (31 fighters, 65 dive-bombers, and 21 torpedo bombers). For the morning search, Fitch devised a plan to cover all contingencies. Because he could not be certain about the movement of the Japanese carriers during the night, he had to assume the possibility that they could still be relatively close by. Therefore,

*Lexington* viewed from *Yorktown* on May 8. Note the Dauntless dive-bombers onboard the *Yorktown*. (US Naval Historical Center)

a full 360-degree search was required which would take 18 SBDs from *Lexington*'s VS-2 and VB-2. The northern part of the search pattern was carried out to 200 miles while the southern part was limited to 125 miles. Upon their return, these 18 aircraft would be devoted to anti-torpedo bomber patrol. Each carrier allocated eight fighters for CAP missions during the day and *Yorktown* dedicated eight SBDs for anti-torpedo bomber patrols. On both carriers, the remaining aircraft were spotted ready to conduct the strike when locating information was received.

During the night of May 7/8, Inoue ordered Takagi to take his carriers to a point 110 miles south-southeast of Rossel Island by dawn to be in position to engage TF-17. However, for a number of reasons, dawn found the MO Carrier Striking Force in a position 140 miles northeast of Rossel Island. Since the failed night strike was so long in returning, the Japanese carriers had to steam to the east to recover aircraft until 2200hrs. Hara advised Takagi to keep heading east or to head south in order to hit the American carriers from the flank. Takagi rejected this recommendation, but did concur with Hara's recommendation to move the MO Carrier Striking Force's dawn position northeast of Rossel Island contrary to Inoue's orders. Hara thought this position would allow him to conduct a more refined search rather than an omni-directional search if he obeyed Takagi's orders and proceeded to the area southeast of Rossel Island, which was close to the last position of the American carriers. Hara's plan meant that fewer aircraft were required to conduct searches and more aircraft were devoted to strike missions.

Hara's aircraft situation on the morning of May 8 was not as favorable as Fitch's. Carrier Division 5 possessed 96 operational aircraft – 38 fighters, 33 carrier bombers and 25 carrier attack planes. Compared with TF-17, the MO Carrier Striking Force could muster 21 fewer aircraft, with the primary difference being the marked American edge in dive-bombers. In contrast to Fitch, Hara's search plan was more austere. According to IJN search doctrine, he preferred to use cruiser floatplanes to conduct search missions saving the carrier aircraft for strike duties. However, on May 8, rough seas prevented the Japanese cruisers from contributing their aircraft. Hara was forced to devote seven carrier attack planes to cover the southern arc from his carriers out to a distance of 250 miles. Four land-based bombers from Rabaul and three flying boats from Tulagi were tasked to search south of the Louisiades.

By 0600hrs, the MO Carrier Striking Force was located some 220 miles northeast of TF-17 under heavy weather. Takagi continued to head north to meet with the cruisers *Kinugasa* and *Furutaka*, detached by Inoue from the MO Main Force to augment the screen of the carrier force. The rest of the elements of the MO operation, including the Main Force, the Invasion Force and the Covering Force, were ordered to gather 40 miles east of Woodlark

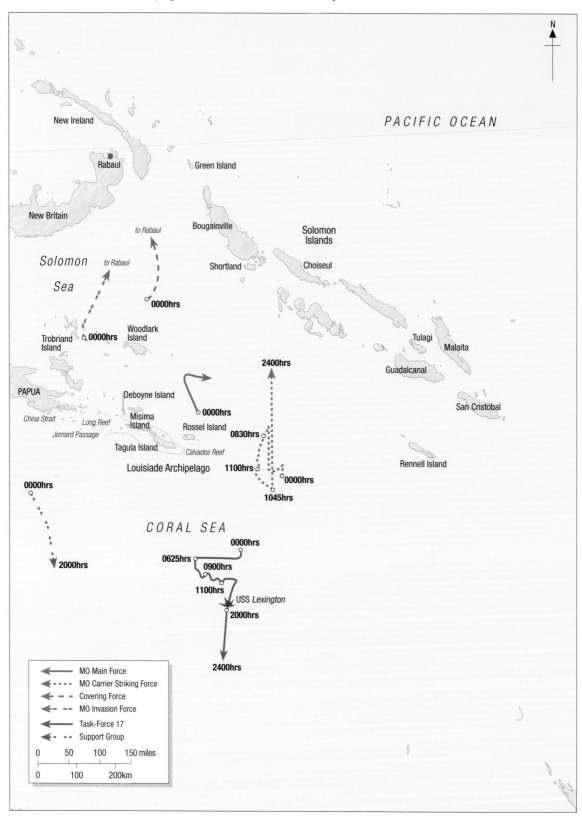

Island in the afternoon. After the MO Striking Force had cleared the way, the convoy would proceed to Port Moresby to conduct the invasion now scheduled for May 12.

Weather played an important role in the events of May 8. The edge of the weather front had moved 30–50 miles to the north and northeast. This brought TF-17 out from under the heavy weather that offered a degree of protection from enemy reconnaissance and placed it in an area of light haze with greatly increased visibility. Conversely, the Japanese carriers now operated in an area of heavy weather with thick clouds and squalls. As later was the case, this made the job of American aviators more difficult.

# THE AMERICAN STRIKE ON THE MO CARRIER STRIKING FORCE

Japanese search aircraft were in the air by 0615hrs, followed by the 18 TF-17 SBDs at 0635hrs. It did not take long for each side to find what they were looking for. The Japanese were the first to have success. At 0802hrs, *Yorktown*'s radar reported a contact 18 miles to the northeast, but TF-17's CAP was unable to find or intercept the snooper. At 0822hrs, a report was issued by the Japanese search plane that two American carriers had been spotted and reported at 235 miles from the MO Striking Force on a bearing of 205 degrees. Radio intelligence units on both *Lexington* and *Yorktown* both confirmed the fact that the Japanese aircraft had spotted TF-17 and had issued a report.

The first report received by Fletcher and Fitch was at 0820hrs when a VS-2 SBD spotted the MO Carrier Striking Force in bad weather. When plotted out, the contact was 175 miles from TF-17 on a bearing of 028 degrees and was headed away from the American carriers. At 175 miles, the Japanese carriers were at the edge of the striking range of the TBDs; nevertheless, it was decided to launch a full strike and head TF-17 toward the contact to reduce the distance the strike would have to fly back to their home carriers.

The Americans were the first to get their strikes in the air. At 0900hrs, the *Yorktown* began launching her strike of 39 aircraft (six fighters, 24 dive-bombers and nine torpedo bombers) followed at 0907hrs with a 36-aircraft strike from the *Lexington* (nine fighters, 15 dive-bombers and 12 torpedo bombers). With the air battle now beginning, at 0908hrs Fletcher gave Fitch tactical control of TF-17. By 0925hrs, the two American air groups had departed the area of TF-17 to proceed to strike the Japanese. Per American doctrine, the two air groups were widely separated with no single strike

*Shokaku* under attack by dive-bombers from *Yorktown*. *Shokaku* is making a high speed starboard turn in an effort to spoil the aim of her attackers. Note the virtual lack of anti-aircraft fire and the absence of any nearby Japanese escort ships. (US Naval Historical Center)

*Shokaku* shown at high speed conducting a series of sharp evasive turns under attack by *Yorktown* dive-bombers. A large fire can be clearly seen burning fiercely in the bow section of the ship. The heavy black smoke amidships suggests that *Shokaku* has also been hit by the second 1,000-pound bomb scored by *Yorktown's* Dauntlesses, which struck near the island and started large fires on the flight and hangar decks. (US Naval Historical Center)

commander. Additional reports from a VS-2 aircraft at 0934hrs placed the Japanese carriers 191 miles from TF-17. Immediately after recovering his morning reconnaissance aircraft, Fitch planned to head to the northeast to reduce the distance to the Japanese carriers.

When the *Yorktown* strike arrived in the area of the MO Carrier Striking Force, the Japanese force was separated into two sections. *Zuikaku*, escorted by *Myoko* and *Haguro* and three destroyers, was some 11,000yds ahead of the *Shokaku* with her two cruisers, the *Furutaka* and *Kinugasa*, trailing another 11,000yds astern. As the dive-bombers maneuvered into position for attack, the *Zuikaku* group disappeared into a squall. Only a single fighter from the *Yorktown* group even saw *Zuikaku*. *Shokaku*, remaining in an area of clear visibility, took the brunt of *Yorktown's* attack. The 24 SBDs scored two hits with 1,000-pound bombs. The first hit on the port bow started a fire in the forecastle. The second hit the starboard side of the ship near the island and started fires on the flight and hangar decks. The attack of VT-5 was completely futile with all nine torpedoes being dropped too far from their target and all missing. Japanese CAP aircraft and anti-aircraft fire proved to be almost totally ineffective. Two SBDs were lost, but VF-42 Wildcats shot down two Type 0 fighters attempting to prevent VT-5's unsuccessful attack.

A view taken from a Devastator from VT-5 of the attack on *Shokaku* on May 8. *Yorktown's* air group delivered a well-coordinated attack, but achieved only two bomb hits. None of the nine Devastators that dropped their torpedoes scored a hit. (US Naval Historical Center)

Some 30 minutes after the start of *Yorktown*'s attack, *Lexington*'s attack commenced. Storms had scattered *Lexington*'s strike, and the overall results were even more disappointing than *Yorktown*'s. Most of *Lexington*'s dive-bombers missed their target altogether in the bad weather. Only the dive-bomber command element with four SBDs under Commander Ault found a target. All attacked *Shokaku* scoring another 1,000-pound bomb hit. Once again, all torpedo aircraft went after *Shokaku*, and once again her skipper was able to successfully dodge all 11 torpedoes aimed at her. Losses again were light with three fighters and one SBD being shot down. Another fighter and two SBDs, including Commander Ault's, did not find their way back to *Lexington*. Of the 13 total Type 0 fighters assigned to CAP, two were shot down and one damaged by Wildcats. In return, the Japanese fighters accounted for two SBDs and three Wildcats.

The net result of the American strike was disappointing. *Zuikaku*, hidden by clouds, was unscathed. Damage to *Shokaku*, in the form of three 1,000-pound bomb hits, was severe, but she was in no danger of sinking. Casualties totaled 109 dead and another 114 wounded. While the fires aboard *Shokaku* were quickly extinguished, the damage left her unable to operate aircraft. She was ordered to depart the area at 30 knots under the escort of two destroyers.

## THE JAPANESE STRIKE TF-17

On board *Shokaku* and *Zuikaku*, 18 Type 0 fighters, 33 Type 99 carrier bombers and 18 Type 97 carrier attack planes equipped with torpedoes were spotted in readiness. After the 0822hrs contact report, the entire strike was launched under command of Lieutenant-Commander Takahashi. Unlike American doctrine, the entire force departed at 0930hrs and proceeded in a single group under the control of Takahashi. Takagi followed his strike group south at 30 knots. Had he maintained his position, it would have been unlikely that any of the short-ranged American TBDs would have been able even to reach the area of the Japanese carrier force.

Awaiting the Japanese strike was TF-17 with its two carriers, five cruisers and seven destroyers. Fully expecting a Japanese morning attack, Fitch had done his best to mount a robust CAP. Eight Wildcats were already aloft

A somewhat indistinct but compelling photo of *Lexington* as seen from one of the attacking Japanese aircraft. *Lexington* is already burning and the number of splashes around the ship suggests this shot was taken during the dive-bombing attack. (US Naval Historical Center)

## THE AMERICAN CARRIER AIR ATTACK ON *SHOKAKU* ON MAY 8 (pp. 74–75)

Only one of the MO Carrier Striking Force's two carriers was attacked by American aircraft during the carrier battle of May 8, 1942. This scene shows *Shokaku* (**1**) in the midst of the attack by *Yorktown*'s dive-bombers. VS-5 has already conducted its attack with no result. Now it was the turn of VB-5. As *Shokaku*'s captain conducted evasive maneuvers at flank speed, the aircraft from VB-5 pressed their dives to 2,000ft before dropping their weapons. The first hit was scored at 1105hrs when a 1,000-pound bomb hit the flight deck on the port side forward. This created a massive fire that is already evident (**2**). Among the final group of VB-5 Dauntlesses was Lieutenant John Powers who was determined to score a hit on the frantically maneuvering Japanese carrier. During his dive, Powers' aircraft was hit by 20mm fire from an attacking Type 0 fighter, which set the wing of the Dauntless on fire (**3**). Undeterred, Powers pressed his dive to under 1,000ft before dropping. His bomb scored a critical hit on the starboard side adjacent to the island creating massive fires on the flight and hangar decks. This hit ensured the *Shokaku* could no longer operate aircraft and would be unable to continue in the battle. Powers attempted to pull out of his dive at 200 feet but was unsuccessful and splashed near his intended target. For his undoubted determination and bravery, he was awarded the Medal of Honor posthumously.

Unlike the damage caused by the two bombs that hit the ship, the two torpedoes that hit *Lexington* caused major structural damage. This view was taken on May 8 after the morning torpedo attack and shows the port side looking aft. Seen clearly is the damage caused by the torpedo that hit the ship amidships. Note the torn netting that was fitted on the flight deck level. (US Naval Historical Center)

supported by 18 SBDs on anti-torpedo plane duty. At 1055hrs, radars on *Lexington* and *Yorktown* reported a large group of aircraft at 68 miles on a bearing of 020 degrees. Immediately, nine more Wildcats and five additional SBDs were launched. The nine new Wildcats were ordered to proceed down the line of bearing to intercept the Japanese aircraft as far as possible from TF-17. The result of this outer air battle was not favorable for the Americans. The aircraft assigned to intercept the Japanese dive-bombers failed to do so until

*Lexington* during the torpedo bomber phase of the Japanese air attack on May 8. Note the anti-aircraft fire and the Type 97 carrier attack plane visible off the ship's port side. (US Naval Historical Center)

77

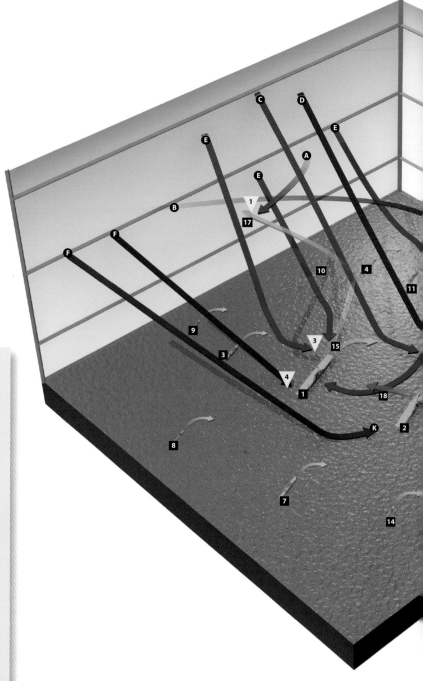

**JAPANESE FORCES:**
**A** *Shokaku* Fighter Unit (nine A6M Zero fighters)
**B** *Zuikaku* Fighter Unit (nine A6M Zero fighters)
**C** *Shokaku* Carrier Bomber Unit
(19 D3A carrier bombers)
**D** *Zuikaku* Carrier Bomber Unit
(14 D3A carrier bombers)
**E** *Shokaku* Carrier Attack Unit
(ten B5N Carrier Attack Planes)
**F** *Zuikaku* Carrier Attack Unit
(eight B5N Carrier Attack Planes)

**AMERICAN FORCES:**
**1** *Lexington*
**2** *Yorktown*
**3** *Minneapolis*
**4** *New Orleans*
**5** *Portland*
**6** *Astoria*
**7** *Chester*
**8** *Phelps*
**9** *Dewey*
**10** *Morris*
**11** *Anderson*
**12** *Russell*
**13** *Hammann*
**14** *Aylwin*
**15** VF-2 CAP (four F4F))
**16** VF-42 CAP (four F4F)
**17** VF-2 CAP augmentation (five F4F)
**18** VF-42 CAP augmentation (four F4F)

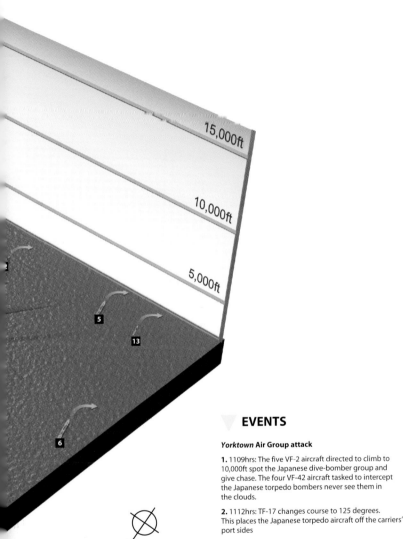

15,000ft

10,000ft

5,000ft

**5**

**13**

**6**

N

## ▼ EVENTS

### Yorktown Air Group attack

**1.** 1109hrs: The five VF-2 aircraft directed to climb to 10,000ft spot the Japanese dive-bomber group and give chase. The four VF-42 aircraft tasked to intercept the Japanese torpedo bombers never see them in the clouds.

**2.** 1112hrs: TF-17 changes course to 125 degrees. This places the Japanese torpedo aircraft off the carriers' port sides

### The Japanese torpedo Attacks

**3.** Fourteen B5Ns are ordered to attack *Lexington* and four to attack *Yorktown*. The main group, escorted by 15 A6Ms, approaches *Lexington* at 4,000ft and attempts to place her in an anvil attack. Ten rush straight at the ship and four from *Zuikaku* attempt to swing around and place *Lexington* in a pincer. VF-2 fighters dive on the torpedo planes and destroy one. The VS-5 SBDs are caught by six *Zuikaku* A6Ms and four are destroyed.

The thirteen remaining B5Ns headed toward the *Lexington* divide into four groups. Fifteen *Lexington* SBDs are deployed at 2,000ft altitude 3,000yds from *Lexington*. With only three A6Ms remaining to protect the B5Ns, the nine VS-2 SBDs on the port side are in a good position to intercept the torpedo planes. Two B5Ns are shot down, but 15 of 18 torpedo planes get through the American CAP

1118hrs: lookouts on *Yorktown* spot four B5Ns from *Zuikaku* off the port bow. *Yorktown* makes a starboard turn to keep her stern to the torpedo planes. One B5N launches torpedo and is shot down after launch.

1119hrs: the other three aircraft launch at 500yds but all miss along the *Yorktown*'s port side. Another B5N is shot down.

1118hrs: *Lexington* faces a pincer attack with three *Zuikaku* B5Ns and two *Shokaku* B5Ns curving around the port bow. The Japanese torpedo planes are at 150ft altitude trying to find gaps through the screen. If Captain Sherman turns *Lexington* into one group of aircraft to comb the tracks of their torpedoes, the other group will have a clear shot. Sherman decides to execute a port turn in order to present stern to the group of three *Zuikaku* aircraft. All three miss and the two *Shokaku* launch their torpedoes from the starboard side, but both miss astern *Lexington*.

Seven more B5Ns remain on *Lexington*'s port side. Sherman orders a hard turn to starboard to turn away from the threat. However, *Lexington* is slow to respond. The most northern group of two B5Ns veer off to attack the cruiser *Minneapolis*; both torpedoes miss. Only four more B5Ns remain to deal a serious blow to *Lexington*. The Japanese aircraft close to 700yds and then drop their weapons from 250ft. The first pair runs deep and passes under *Lexington*.

1120hrs: the first torpedo hit is taken on the forward port side. This is followed by another hit under the island.

### The dive-bomb attacks on *Lexington*

**4.** 1121hrs: 19 *Shokaku* D3As dive from 14,000ft on *Lexington*. In the face of increasingly heavy antiaircraft fire, the dive-bombers reach 1500ft and drop their weapons. *Lexington* is barraged by near misses, but only two bombs hit. Both cause minor damage. The last two dive-bombers abort their dives on *Lexington* and go for *Yorktown*; both miss. Of the 19 D3As, one is destroyed by anti-aircraft fire and one is shot down by fighters.

### The dive-bomb attacks on *Yorktown*

**5.** 1124hrs: 14 *Zuikaku* dive-bombers begin their attack from 13,000ft.

1127hrs: A 250kg semi-armor-piercing bomb hits the center of the flight deck forward of the middle elevator. Because of the attacks by the two defending Wildcats, good ship-handling by Captain Buckmaster, and a difficult crosswind dive, this is the only hit scored. Several near misses also cause damage including a bomb amidships on the port side that opens fuel bunkers to the sea.

# THE JAPANESE CARRIER AIRCRAFT ATTACK ON THE AMERICAN CARRIERS *LEXINGTON* AND *YORKTOWN*

they had already commenced their dives and the Wildcats assigned to intercept the low-flying torpedo planes missed them in the clouds. Takahashi took his 33 dive-bombers to a position upwind from TF-17 while the 18 torpedo planes were ordered to conduct an immediate attack.

Of the 18 Type 97 carrier attack planes, 14 were assigned to attack *Lexington* with only four remaining to attack *Yorktown*. Despite the efforts of the defending Wildcats and the large numbers of SBDs conducting patrols against the slower torpedo planes, 15 of the 18 Type 97s survived the CAP to launch attacks. The four allocated to attack *Yorktown* all missed for the loss of two aircraft. With 14 Type 97s available to attack *Lexington*, and the limited maneuverability of the huge ship, the Japanese achieved much better results. With sufficient aircraft to mount an anvil attack, Captain Sherman could not avoid all of the nine torpedoes aimed at *Lexington*. After deftly avoiding the first five torpedoes launched from two groups attacking from each beam of the ship, the last group of four Type 97s had a clear shot. Two

This view is of *Lexington*'s forward port side 5in./25 gun gallery. The first bomb to hit the ship exploded here, destroying the gun and causing severe personnel casualties. (US Naval Historical Center)

torpedoes ran deep under *Lexington*'s keel, but the final two scored hits on the port side. The first, at 1120hrs, hit forward and jammed the two elevators in the raised position. More importantly, it buckled the port aviation fuel tank and caused small cracks. In turn, this caused gasoline vapors to spread. The second hit was scored under the island near the firerooms. Three filled with water forcing three boilers to be shut down. Several fuel bunkers were opened to the sea, which created a large oil slick. The second hit caused a six to seven degree list, but movement of liquids inside the ship quickly corrected this.

Takahashi's orders for the dive-bombers to take a position upwind placed them several minutes behind the torpedo attack. He ordered 19 dive-bombers from *Shokaku* to deal with *Lexington* with the balance of the dive-bombers from *Zuikaku* to attack *Yorktown*. Escorting Type 0 fighters were successful in protecting the carrier bombers from American fighter interception, so

A Type 97 carrier attack plane going down in flames on May 8. During the actual attack on TF-17, an ineffectual American fighter interception and relatively ineffective anti-aircraft fire translated into low losses for Japanese torpedo aircraft. However, overall losses of Japanese torpedo planes were catastrophic. (US Naval Historical Center)

## THE JAPANESE CARRIER AIR ATTACK OF MAY 8 AGAINST *LEXINGTON* (pp. 82–83)

Within minutes of the successful torpedo attack on *Lexington* (**1**), the ship was subjected to an intense dive-bombing attack from 19 *Shokaku* Type 99 carrier bombers. These dive-bombers began their attack at 14,000ft unmolested by defending American fighters. In turn, each Type 99 braved increasingly heavy anti-aircraft fire and dove to within 1,500ft of its target before dropping its weapons. Despite their determination, the Japanese were not rewarded for their efforts. Of 17 bombs dropped against *Lexington*, only two hit. Both of these caused only minor damage. The first hit the forward corner of the flight deck on the port side and knocked out the Number 6 5in. gun causing severe personnel casualties. The second bomb landed on the port side of the massive smokestack but caused little damage, though it did cause further personnel casualties among the crews manning nearby anti-aircraft weapons. This scene depicts the opening of the attack before either hit had been scored. Many near misses were scored, as seen in this view (**2**), and some of these caused damage to *Lexington's* hull.

all 33 delivered attacks on their targets. Despite bravely pressing their attacks against increasingly heavy anti-aircraft fire, the results were very disappointing for the Japanese. Both American carriers were deluged in a series of near misses, but only a total of three bombs hit their targets. Against *Lexington*, two *Shokaku* dive-bombers scored direct hits. Both inflicted minor damage. The first hit the forward corner of the flight deck knocking out the forward 5in. sponson on the port side. The second hit the port side of the massive smoke stack causing little damage but inflicting casualties on nearby anti-aircraft gun crews. Two Type 99 carrier bombers were destroyed in the attack.

Against *Yorktown*, a combination of attacks by two defending Wildcats, good ship handling by Captain Buckmaster and a crosswind drop meant the 14 *Zuikaku* dive-bombers scored only a single hit. The single 550-pound semi-armor-piercing bomb hit the center of the flight deck forward of the middle elevator. It penetrated four decks before exploding where it killed the personnel of a repair party and caused structural damage. The resulting fire produced dense smoke that issued through the small hole left in the flight deck. The damage forced the temporary evacuation of three firerooms reducing speed to 25 knots. Several of the near misses were damaging. Another 550-pound bomb exploded amidships on the port side and was close enough to open several fuel bunkers to the sea creating a large oil slick.

The Japanese strike had not been as devastating as the Americans had expected. *Yorktown*'s crew had quickly put out the fires and the firerooms were re-manned bringing her speed up to 28 knots. Even *Lexington*, recipient of much greater damage, seemed to be battleworthy and in no danger of sinking. After the strike, Takahashi radioed back at 1125hrs that a *Saratoga*-class carrier had sunk as a result of nine torpedo hits and ten bomb hits. The *Yorktown* was damaged as a result of a claimed two torpedo hits and eight to ten bomb hits.

Despite the efforts of 20 Wildcats and 23 SBDs on CAP, Japanese losses were relatively light. The combined CAP, together with anti-aircraft fire accounted for an apparent total of five dive-bombers and eight torpedo planes. The cost to the Americans was three fighters and five SBDs. However, many Japanese aircraft were damaged resulting in the ditching of another seven aircraft en route to their carriers and another 12 were jettisoned owing to damage after they had landed. Returning VF-42 escorts from the *Yorktown* strike accounted for two additional Japanese aircraft, both noteworthy. One was the carrier attack plane that had spotted TF-17 and shadowed the American carriers for over an hour without having been spotted by the American CAP. The second was strike leader Takahashi, the leader of the *Shokaku* air group since Pearl Harbor.

*Lexington* viewed from the heavy cruiser *Portland* after the carrier has recovered her strike against the Japanese MO Carrier Striking Force. The ship remains operational despite taking two torpedo hits and two bomb hits from Japanese carrier aircraft. However, *Lexington* is clearly down by the bow, a result of the first torpedo hit. This view clearly shows the ship's Coral Sea armament fit. In place of the 8in. gunhouses, 1.1in. quad mounts have been fitted and additional 20mm guns are also evident, including on a platform fitted at the base of the massive stack. (US Naval Historical Center)

## AFTER THE STRIKES

Both the Japanese and American air groups had been shattered by events of May 8. After both strikes had been recovered in the early afternoon, neither was in a position to resume the battle immediately. *Yorktown*'s strike returned at 1300hrs, but after recovery only 12 SBDs and eight TBDs were operational and only seven torpedoes remained in the *Yorktown*'s magazines for future strikes by VT-5. *Lexington*'s strike returned beginning at 1322hrs, but after an explosion at 1247hrs in the forward part of the ship, her condition looked uncertain. Given the uncertainty over the condition of *Lexington*, the condition of *Yorktown*'s air group (especially with regard to fighters) and the growing concern with TF-17's fuel status since the loss of *Neosho*, Fletcher proposed at 1315hrs that TF-17 retire to the south. Fitch concurred at 1324hrs.

At this point, the battle of Coral Sea was effectively over, but the reckoning for the US Navy was not done. The torpedo damage to *Lexington* proved mortal. The first torpedo hit outboard of the aviation gasoline tanks had transmitted the shock of the blast to the tanks and created cracks in the seams allowing vapors to escape. By 1247hrs, these vapors had reached the motor generators in the ship's internal communications room, which caused an explosion and fires in the forward part of the ship. Damage control parties could not control the spread of the fires and further massive explosions occurred at 1442hrs and 1525hrs. At 1707hrs, Captain Sherman decided to abandon ship before darkness made the rescue of the crew more difficult. *Lexington* was later scuttled by destroyer torpedoes and finally sank at 1952hrs.

The plight of the MO Carrier Striking Force was only marginally better. The damaged *Shokaku* had been escorted out of the area, and *Zuikaku* was ordered to recover all returning strike aircraft. Between 1310hrs and 1410hrs, 46 aircraft were recovered. Of these, 12 were pushed over the side and another seven ditched before they could land. At 1430hrs, a total of nine strike aircraft were operational aboard *Zuikaku*. Accordingly, Takagi informed Inoue that a second strike was impossible. The Carrier Striking Force headed north at 1500hrs to depart the battle area and to address the fuel situation that had become desperate, with some destroyers down to 20 percent of capacity.

The failure of the Carrier Striking Force to crush the American carriers meant the end of the MO Operation. On the morning of May 8, Inoue had ordered all forces not involved in the carrier battle to move northeast. That morning, search aircraft from Rabaul had also reported an Allied force of

The heavy cruiser *Aoba* played a frustrating role at the Coral Sea, first unsuccessfully screening *Shoho* and later being moved to screen the MO Carrier Striking Force. (Yamato Museum)

one battleship, two cruisers and four destroyers between the Louisiades and Port Moresby. Inoue's plan to hit this force with land-based bombers from Rabaul was scratched when heavy rains grounded all aircraft at Rabaul. If having an intact Allied force with heavy units blocking his advance to Port Moresby was not bad enough, in the afternoon Inoue was informed of the results of the carrier battle. With *Shokaku* out of the battle and heavy aircraft losses that precluded a second strike, Inoue knew that the prospects for mounting an invasion of Port Moresby were over. At 1545hrs, he ordered all forces to head north; at 1620hrs he postponed the MO Operation and ordered the evacuation of the seaplane base at Deboyne Island.

When Combined Fleet headquarters learned of Inoue's postponement order, Yamamoto took immediate action. At 2200hrs, he ordered Inoue to continue to pursue the American forces and to complete their destruction. In response, Inoue ordered the reoccupation of the Deboyne Base and shifted the remainder of Goto's most powerful remaining units, including his two remaining heavy cruisers and most of the 6th Destroyer Squadron, to join with the Carrier Striking Force. Thus reinforced, the MO Carrier Striking Force spent May 9 refueling, then re-entered the Coral Sea on May 10 to reopen the battle. *Zuikaku*'s operational aircraft had risen to a total of 45 – 24 fighters, 13 carrier bombers and eight carrier attack planes. By dawn on May 10, Takagi was some 340 miles southwest of Tulagi. From this position, he conducted a search but gained no contact. On May 11, the futility of continuing operations was obvious and the Carrier Striking Force moved around San Cristobal Island and headed north.

Like Takagi, Fletcher decided that the best course of action was to retire. MacArthur's aircraft had already reported the northerly movement of the invasion convoy, so Fletcher could safely assume that the threat of invasion at Port Moresby was over. Following the sinking of *Lexington*, he could not risk losing a second of Nimitz's precious carriers, which would have turned the battle into a strategic disaster for the US Navy. For the remainder of May 8, he moved south into the Coral Sea. Fearful of pursuit on May 9, he continued to retire at high speed. When Takagi's remaining carrier attempted to regain contact on May 10, Fletcher was already safely out of the battle area. On May 15, TF-17 anchored at Tongatabu in the Tonga Islands, and from there the *Yorktown* proceeded to Pearl Harbor for repairs. On that same day, Halsey's TF-16 with the carriers *Enterprise* and *Hornet* was spotted by a Type 97 flying boat approximately 450 miles east of Tulagi. These final moves in the battle of Coral Sea were actually the prelude to the battle of Midway, now less than three weeks away.

# THE ACCOUNTING

Not surprisingly, Japanese plans for the ambitious MO Operation proved fragile. Inoue had barely enough forces assigned to him to accomplish his mission, and those that he did have were primarily second-rate units. After the run of successes for the last five months, "victory disease" was alive and well in the Navy General Staff and the Combined Fleet. Both continued to count on a passive enemy who would play his predicted role while an intricate Japanese operation unfolded. Unlike in the first few months of the war when the Japanese had carefully orchestrated their moves to take place under conditions of local air superiority, this was not realistically achievable for the MO Operation. Instead of facing only meager Dutch, British or American land-based air forces where only minimal air protection had sufficed, in May 1942 the IJN planned to conduct a major invasion in the face of an American carrier force backed by large land-based air forces. It was not a formula for success.

Nevertheless, in spite of the fragility of the plans for MO, it did contain the seeds of success, if not against Port Moresby, then against the American carrier force. To Yamamoto, the latter was arguably more important than the former. When the MO Carrier Striking Force rounded the Solomon Islands, it was in a very favorable tactical position to ambush Fletcher's unsuspecting carriers. Here the timidity of Takagi and Hara threw away the best Japanese hope for success. For two key days leading up to the battle's climax, they did not conduct a general search for the American carriers, not wanting to reveal their position. Though the coordination between Japanese land-based naval air forces and their carriers was far better than the coordination between American land-based aviation and carrier forces, it was not good enough to allow Takagi to play such a passive role. On May 6 and again on May 7, the Japanese threw away a chance to launch a devastating blow against Fletcher's carriers. On May 7 in particular, the Americans were very fortunate that Japanese reconnaissance efforts were so unbelievably faulty. Even during the climactic battle on May 8, the IJN's aviators had the best of the exchange owing in no large measure to superior doctrine and coordination. Even after the exchange, Takagi should have realized that the true strategic prize at hand was not Port Moresby, but the American carriers. With this knowledge, he should have relentlessly pursued the second damaged American carrier, as Yamamoto reminded him late on May 8. By any measure, the battle of the Coral Sea was a series of lost opportunities for the Japanese.

For the US Navy, the battle was a close-run affair. When Nimitz saw an opportunity to engage a portion of the Kido Butai on near equal terms, he aggressively seized it. Charged to execute Nimitz's order, Fletcher became fixated on the Japanese forces approaching from his northwest, which included, according to the intelligence he was provided, the Japanese carrier forces. Meanwhile, Fletcher ignored his eastern flank. After paying no price for this neglect on May 6, he was fortunate that the exchange on May 7 against secondary targets went his way and did not bring a full Japanese carrier strike on his force. After taking the brunt of the exchange on May 8, Fletcher was unfortunate that a material defect caused the destruction of *Lexington*. His withdrawal on May 8 with his remaining carrier was undoubtedly the correct decision, as was so profoundly evidenced by *Yorktown*'s pivotal role at Midway a month later.

A burned-out B5N2 Type 97 carrier attack plane on a reef somewhere in the South Pacific after the battle of the Coral Sea. The single white fuselage band indicates that this is an aircraft from *Shokaku*'s air group. Losses for Carrier Division 5 were heavy during the battle, especially in carrier attack planes. Of the 39 Type 97s available on May 6, only eight remained operational on May 10. (US Naval Historical Center)

Both sides paid a high price in the first carrier battle of the Pacific War. The invasion of Port Moresby had been turned away, but the Japanese did add Tulagi to their list of conquests. Losses to the IJN had been high, in fact more severe than any battle to date in the war. The light carrier *Shoho* was sunk, the largest ship lost thus far in the war. In addition, a destroyer and several minor ships were lost in the American carrier raid on Tulagi. Most importantly, the bomb hits on *Shokaku* kept her in the shipyard until July 1942. Carrier aircraft losses were very severe. Exact numbers are difficult to ascertain, but if sources stating that the total number of aircraft remaining (in all conditions) on *Zuikaku* on the evening of May 8 are accurate at 52, then Carrier Division 5 had lost 69 aircraft since May 6. Combined with the loss of *Shoho*'s entire air group (18 aircraft), at least 87 total carrier aircraft were lost. The heavy aircraft losses crippled *Zuikaku*'s air group and meant that she would also be out of action for several months. IJN personnel deaths totaled 1,074.

US losses were highlighted by the loss of *Lexington*, constituting 25 percent of the Pacific Fleet's operational carrier strength. *Yorktown* suffered minor damage, but her survival allowed the Americans to rightfully claim a strategic victory. In addition to *Lexington*, an oiler and a destroyer were sunk. Total carrier aircraft losses stood at 81, 35 of these when *Lexington* sank. American naval dead totaled 543.

Beginning at 1247hrs on May 8, a series of fuel-vapor-induced explosions occurred on *Lexington*. These started fires that could not be extinguished and led to her loss. This view shows one of the major explosions during the carrier's abandonment. Note *Yorktown* on the horizon. (US Naval Historical Center)

# THE AFTERMATH

The Coral Sea has rightly been described as a strategic American victory. For the first time in the war (excepting the temporarily successful defense of Wake Island in December 1941), a Japanese attack had been repulsed. In fact, the Coral Sea could be described as the high water mark of the IJN. With a few minor exceptions, it would make no more advances during the war. The abortive attack on Port Moresby in May 1942 was the best chance the Japanese had of taking the port and airfield and posing a direct threat to Australia. With their seaborne invasion stopped, the Japanese were forced to seek other alternatives to take Port Moresby. Unable to proceed by sea, the Imperial Japanese Army attempted an overland attack in July 1942. This logistically tenuous plan over some of the roughest terrain in the world was doomed to failure.

It has become commonly accepted that the Coral Sea, while an American strategic victory, was also an American tactical defeat. This might be true if the battle is considered in isolation. While sinking only a light carrier and

As soon as *Yorktown* arrived in Pearl Harbor after the Coral Sea, she was rushed into dry dock for repairs to battle damage suffered by Japanese dive-bombing. These frantic efforts resulted in her being made battle ready by May 29 in time for her to depart Pearl Harbor on May 30 to participate in the Midway battle. This contrasts greatly with the overconfident Japanese who made no concerted effort to make even the undamaged *Zuikaku* available for Midway. (US Naval Historical Center)

damaging a fleet carrier, the US Navy lost one of its four operational Pacific Fleet carriers. However, this view lacks credibility as the Coral Sea cannot be examined in isolation. For the Japanese it may have been a subsidiary operation, but its impact was decidedly strategic. Yamamoto's main goal in early 1942 was to attack what he considered to be the American center of gravity in the Pacific – the US Navy, and more specifically its carriers. This was not the aim of the MO Operation, but it was the principal objective of the MI Operation (the codename for the attack on Midway), which was scheduled less than a month after the intended Port Moresby invasion. To conduct the MI Operation successfully, Yamamoto's plan depended on maintaining superiority in fleet carriers. Violating the principle of mass, Yamamoto committed one-third of the Kido Butai's carriers to the MO Operation. Though neither was sunk in the operation, both were removed from his order of battle for the MI Operation. Down to only four carriers, Yamamoto had lost his decisive edge in carriers so necessary to guarantee success for the coming decisive clash with the US Navy. Had the MO Striking Force succeeded in sinking both American carriers in the Coral Sea, the battle could have been considered a Japanese strategic victory, even without the seizure of Port Moresby. The removal of Carrier Division 5 from the Kido Butai made the Coral Sea both a strategic and tactical disaster for the Japanese.

For the Americans, the Coral Sea was a clear-cut victory. Nimitz's decision to send half of his carriers to the South Pacific had paid rich dividends. Not only had Japanese expansion been curbed, but the offensive power of the IJN had been somewhat blunted. All three of the IJN's carriers committed to the battle were either destroyed or rendered inoperative for the next phase of the Pacific War. Nimitz paid a high price for his victory when *Lexington*'s damage proved fatal, but the damage to *Yorktown* was light enough to allow her repair in only days, permitting her to play a role in the Midway battle.

The Coral Sea demonstrated several important themes in 1942 carrier battles that neither side had time to fully digest by the time the most decisive carrier battle of the war took place at Midway a month later. Both sides expected that full enemy attacks would destroy their own carriers. In fact, this did not occur. US Navy striking power was restricted by its continued doctrine of individual strikes mounted by single air groups. Recurring coordination and communications problems made the coherence of these strikes less than guaranteed. The primary striking power of the American

Yorktown survived the Coral Sea and returned to Pearl Harbor on May 27. She is shown here arriving with her crew mustered at quarters. Yorktown immediately went into dry dock to repair battle damage and departed May 30 to take part in the battle of Midway. The mainmast of the sunken battleship Arizona is visible in the distance just right of Yorktown's stern. (US Naval Historical Center)

carriers was its dive-bombers. The TBD's performance at the Coral Sea hid its true vulnerability. At Midway, it would be shockingly revealed. The Japanese air groups had shown themselves to be formidable offensive weapons. The key to their success was torpedo attacks. Japanese bombs were relatively small and lacked the power of the 1,000-pound bombs carried on the Dauntless. However, the combination of the Type 97 carrier attack plane and its dependable air-launched torpedo was a deadly ship-killer as proven by Lexington's eventual loss to damage resulting from aircraft torpedoes. The abortive Japanese night attack on May 7 proved key as it removed sufficient torpedo aircraft from the Japanese strike on May 8 to devote any more than four torpedo planes against Yorktown. Had the Japanese placed even a single torpedo hit on Yorktown, history would have been altered. Even if she survived the battle, such damage certainly would not have been repaired in time for her to take part in the Midway battle.

The strikes of May 8 had shown that the defensive power of both carrier forces was lacking. Both sides lacked sufficient fighters to mount effective CAP while providing strike escort. Anti-aircraft fire was equally ineffective in protecting the carriers. Especially ineffective were the defensive efforts of the Japanese whose anti-aircraft fire was totally useless. Japanese CAP was nearly as bad, especially against dive-bombers. These were lessons the

Yorktown on June 4, 1942, shown listing to port dead in the water after being torpedoed by Japanese aircraft. Though she survived the Coral Sea with only a single bomb hit, Yorktown could not survive the combination of bombs and torpedoes suffered at Midway. (US Naval Historical Center)

Japanese would learn much more clearly at Midway. American defensive efforts were lackluster at the Coral Sea, but would improve in each carrier battle of 1942. The huge potential advantage of using radar for fighter direction was unrealized at the Coral Sea, but with experience, would become a major factor in providing real air defense of the carriers. At the Coral Sea, anti-aircraft gunnery was ineffective in preventing attacks, but did inflict real attrition on Japanese strike aircraft. As long as the Japanese had well-trained pilots they could press home attacks on carriers and inflict damage, sometimes fatal. However, by the end of 1942, attrition of Japanese strike aircraft by gunnery and fighters became prohibitive.

After the Coral Sea, another three carrier battles were fought during the remainder of 1942. All of these were overshadowed by the battle of Midway in June during which the Kido Butai's four active carriers were all sunk. In return, the US Navy lost only the quickly repaired *Yorktown*. Even after Midway, the IJN's rebuilt carrier force still possessed a numerical advantage over the US Navy's carrier force. In two carrier battles fought in the fiercely contested waters around Guadalcanal, the IJN's carrier force, now centered around the *Shokaku* and *Zuikaku*, performed well, sinking the carrier *Hornet* and losing only a light carrier in return. At the end of 1942, both sides' carrier forces were exhausted. However, American shipyards were busy changing the naval balance. Beginning in 1943, 14 *Essex*-class carriers entered service before the end of the war. With these fine ships and new aircraft and a breed of highly trained aviators, the carrier war entered a new phase. In the last carrier battles of the war, the *Shokaku* and *Zuikaku* finally met their ends. The *Shokaku* was sunk in history's largest carrier battle in June 1944 at the battle of the Philippine Sea. The *Zuikaku* was sacrificed at the battle of Leyte Gulf in October 1944. The turning of the Japanese tide begun at the Coral Sea led eventually to Japan's surrender in August 1945.

After its uncertain beginning at the Coral Sea, the US Navy's Fast Carrier Force developed into a tool for victory in the Pacific War. Six of the 14 *Essex*-class carriers that saw combat during the war are shown in this December 1944 shot together with several *Independence*-class light carriers. Among those present was the USS *Lexington* (CV-16), named for the carrier lost at the Coral Sea. She is identifiable by her dark blue Measure 21 camouflage scheme. (US Naval Historical Center)

# FURTHER READING

The Coral Sea has long been overshadowed by the battle of Midway by historians. Few accounts have been written devoted solely to the Coral Sea and a definitive account of the battle has yet to appear. The titles below are recommended for additional research into the battle.

Bullard, Steven (translator), *Japanese Army Operations in the South Pacific Area* Australian War Memorial: Canberra, 2007. Despite the title of this work, it is a very valuable resource for the events leading up to the Coral Sea as it contains excerpts from two volumes of the official Japanese history of the Pacific War (*Senshi Sosho*). This is the first translation of the *Senshi Sosho* series available to anyone other than a few historians who have had parts of *Senshi Sosho* privately translated.

Dull, Paul S, *A Battle History of the Imperial Japanese Navy 1941–45* Naval Institute Press: Annapolis, MD, 1978. One of the first American scholars to heavily use Japanese sources.

Lundstrom, John B., *The First Team* Naval Institute Press: Annapolis, MD, 1984

——, *Black Shoe Carrier Admiral* Naval Institute Press: Annapolis, MD, 2006. Lundstrom is one of the finest historians of the Pacific War working today. *The First Team* is devoted to the early stages of the carrier war and includes detailed accounts of the air battle at the Coral Sea. In addition to exhaustive research into US Navy sources, Lundstrom makes good use of Japanese sources (including *Senshi Sosho*) thus presenting a balanced view of the battle. His newest book, *Black Shoe Carrier Admiral*, includes an examination of the Coral Sea from the perspective of Jack Fletcher. This is perhaps the best-balanced and most original account of the battle available.

Millot, Bernard, *The Battle of the Coral Sea* Ian Allan: London, 1974. This is one of the first books on the battle and remains useful.

Morison, Samuel Eliot, *Coral Sea, Midway and Submarine Actions May 1942–August 1942* (*Volume IV of The History of United States Naval Operations in World War II*) Little, Brown and Company: Boston, MA, 1975. Morison's work was the best account available of the battle for many years being originally published in 1949. It must now be used with caution, from its dated order of battle to its scathing treatment of Fletcher.

Willmott, H. P., *The Barrier and the Javelin*, Naval Institute Press: Annapolis, MD, 1983. A thoughtful account of the Pacific War from February to June 1942 that includes coverage of the Coral Sea and Midway. The best work available for placing the battle into an overall context of the war.

Additionally, the following Osprey titles are useful for additional background:

Stille, Mark, New Vanguard 109: *Imperial Japanese Navy Aircraft Carriers 1921–45* Osprey Publishing Ltd: Oxford, 2005

——, New Vanguard 114: *US Navy Aircraft Carriers 1922–45 (Prewar classes)* Osprey Publishing Ltd: Oxford, 2005

——, Duel 6: *USN Carriers vs IJN Carriers* Osprey Publishing Ltd: Oxford, 2007

# INDEX